Logistics

U.S. Marine Corps

DEPARTMENT OF THE NAVY
Headquarters United States Marine Corps
Washington, DC 20380-1775

21 February 1997

FOREWORD

Marine Corps Doctrinal Publication (MCDP) 4, *Logistics*, describes the theory and philosophy of military logistics as practiced by the United States Marine Corps. It provides all Marines a conceptual framework for the understanding and practice of effective logistics. The Marine Corps' view of logistics is based on our common understanding of the nature of war and on our warfighting philosophy as described in MCDP 1, *Warfighting*.

Our doctrine recognizes that logistics is an integral part of warfighting. Logistics provides the resources of combat power, brings those resources to the battle, and sustains them throughout the course of operations. Our approach to logistics recognizes that war is conducted in an environment of complexity, fluidity, disorder, and uncertainty and seeks to provide the commander with the physical means to win in this environment. Our logistic capabilities extend our operational limits, allowing us to anticipate requirements while remaining flexible, adaptable, and responsive to changing conditions in the battlespace.

Chapter 1 is based upon the assumption that in order to develop an effective philosophy of logistics, we must first develop a realistic understanding of the nature of logistics. Based upon this understanding, chapter 2 discusses the theoretical aspects of logistics. Building upon the conclusions of the preceding chapters, chapter 3 describes the basic approach of the Marine Corps to logistics.

MCDP 4, *Logistics*, does not supersede any current doctrinal publication. It provides the authoritative basis for the subsequent development of logistic doctrine, education, training, equipment, procedures, and organization. *Logistics* affords no specific techniques or procedures for logistic activities; rather, it offers broad guidance which requires judgment in its application. Other publications in the logistics series of Marine Corps warfighting publications provide specific tactics, techniques, and procedures.

Marine Corps logistic doctrine applies across the full spectrum of conflict from peacekeeping or humanitarian assistance operations on one hand to general war on the other. Furthermore, this publication pertains equally to small-unit leaders and senior commanders. Since logistics is an essential component of any military activity, this publication is meant to guide Marines at all levels of command in both the operating forces and the supporting establishment.

C. C. KRULAK
General, U.S. Marine Corps
Commandant of the Marine Corps

DISTRIBUTION: 142 000003 00

Logistics

Chapter 3. Creating Effective Logistics

The Challenge to Logistics—Maneuver Warfare–*Centers of Gravity and Critical Vulnerabilities–Focus of Effort and the Main Effort–Tempo–Commander's Intent*—Marine Logistics–*Core Capabilities–Planning–Command and Control*—Building Capabilities–*Leadership–Discipline–Attention to Detail–Responsiveness–Doctrine–Education–Training–Procedures–Organization–Equipment and Technology*—Conclusion

Notes

Chapter 1

The Nature of Logistics

"Throughout the struggle, it was in his logistic inability to maintain his armies in the field that the enemy's fatal weakness lay. Courage his forces had in full measure, but courage was not enough. Reinforcements failed to arrive, weapons, ammunition and food alike ran short, and the dearth of fuel caused their powers of tactical mobility to dwindle to the vanishing point. In the last stages of the campaign they could do little more than wait for the Allied advance to sweep over them."[1]

—Dwight Eisenhower

"As we select our forces and plan our operations, ... [w]e must understand how logistics can impact on our concepts of operation. . . . Commanders must base all their concepts of operations on what they know they can do logistically."[2]

—A. M. Gray, Jr.

To conduct logistics effectively, we must first understand its fundamental nature—its purpose and its characteristics—as well as its relationship to the conduct of military operations. This understanding will become the basis for developing a theory of logistics and a practical guide to its application.

WHAT IS LOGISTICS?

Logistics is the science of planning and carrying out the movement and maintenance of forces.[3] Logistics provides the resources of combat power, positions those resources on the battlefield, and sustains them throughout the execution of operations. Logistics encompasses a wide range of actions and the relationships among those actions, as well as the resources that make those actions possible. These actions are all given purpose and definition by the larger art of war, of which logistics is a critical and inseparable part.

Actions that fall into the category of logistics are both humble and magnificent, include both the simple and the complex, and range in size from the tiny to the gargantuan. They include the serving of a single meal, the effective distribution of tens of thousands of separate spare parts, and the movement of vast armadas from one corner of the globe to another. The common thread that unites these otherwise disparate activities is their relationship to the physical needs of a military force. Any action that serves to transport a military force from one place to another, provide it with the physical means of waging war, or preserve its combat power for subsequent employment belongs properly to the realm of logistics.

Logistics can also be described as the bridge which connects a nation's economy to its warfighting forces. *Logistics provides the means which translates national resources into combat power.* Logistics transforms manpower, natural resources, and industrial capacity into units, weapons, equipment, and supplies. It delivers these elements to the theater of operations at the time and place dictated by operational requirements. It sustains the military forces throughout the course of operations. It returns those forces to their home bases when operations are concluded, rearming and reequiping them as needed in preparation for the next action.

The term "logistics" is also used to describe activities in the civilian or commercial world. In this usage, logistics describes the process of procurement, maintenance, distribution, and replacement of resources conducted by corporations, firms, or industries. These activities have many points in common with military logistics and can serve as a source of concepts, techniques, and technologies of great interest to military logisticians. Nonetheless, civilian logistics lacks the warlike purpose that defines military logistics and is thus fundamentally different. In this publication, the term "logistics" therefore describes military logistics.

The terms "logistics" and "combat service support" are often used interchangeably, but there is a distinction. "Logistics" is the larger of the two concepts. Logistics encompasses all actions required to move and maintain forces. This includes the acquisition and positioning of resources as well as the delivery of those resources to the forces. "Combat service support" is the *activity* which actually provides services and supplies to the combat forces. Since most of the delivery of resources occurs at the tactical level of war, combat service support has been considered to be essentially the same as tactical logistics. Indeed, Marine tactical units have logistics officers and logistics sections, but the units that perform logistics functions for these units are referred to as combat service support elements. However, some combat service support is conducted at the operational and strategic levels. For example, health services are provided at the strategic and operational levels through the use of hospital ships, fleet hospitals, and permanent military medical facilities. Conversely, some limited aspects of tactical logistics do not directly correspond to combat service support. (See figure 1, page 6.)

HOW IMPORTANT IS LOGISTICS?

Logistics is part and parcel of any attempt to conduct military operations. It is critical to the creation, maintenance, deployment, and employment of forces as well as to the redeployment, reconstitution, and regeneration of those forces after

5

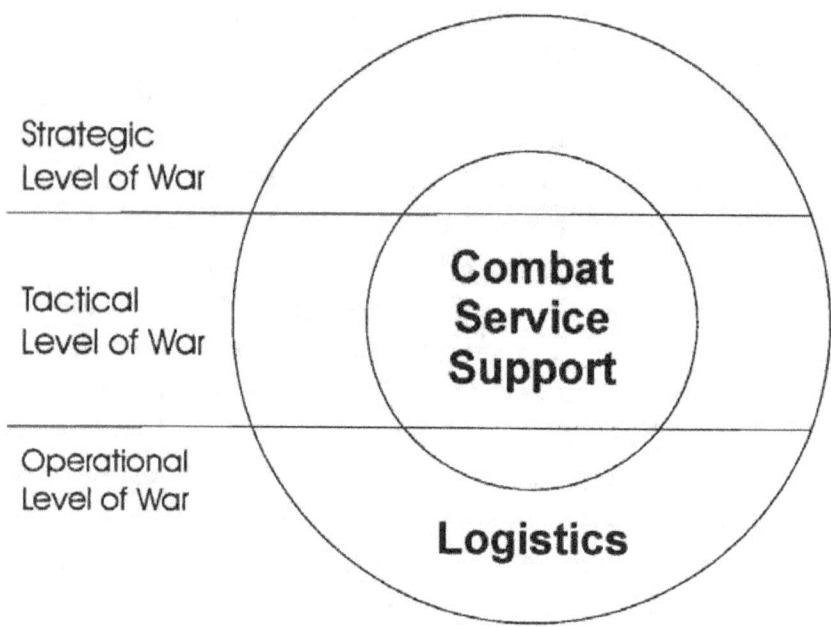

Figure 1. Logistics and combat service support.

their employment. Without logistics, war as a deliberate, organized activity would be impossible. Without logistics, military units cannot be raised or equipped. Without logistics, forces cannot reach the battlefield. Without logistics, weapons go without ammunition, vehicles go without fuel, equipment breaks and stands idle, the sick and wounded go untreated, troops go without food, shelter, and clothing. Thus, *logistics establishes limits on what is operationally possible.* Nevertheless, while logistics sets the limits, the goal of our logistics effort is to extend those limits as far as possible.

Logistics plays a significant role in any military action, whether the action is part of a war, a military operation other than war, or even a training exercise. Whenever military units are employed, they must be deployed and sustained. In fact, logistic activities are conducted much the same way in peace as they are in war or military operations other than war. Unlike certain functions which are conducted only in war, logistics is always "on."

Logistics is concerned with the provision and allocation of resources. The conduct of war or military operations other than war normally requires extensive resources. However, the resources available to create and sustain combat power are almost always limited. Demand usually exceeds supply. *Logistics helps to ensure the effective use of limited resources.* Logistics assists the commander in making best use of the available resources to accomplish the mission.

Logistics by itself cannot win wars, but it has been the major contributing factor in losing many wars, particularly in the 20th century. At the strategic level, the inability of a nation to generate sufficient forces, move them to the front, and support them once engaged invariably leads to deterioration of the forces' material condition, morale, and tactical capability. This deterioration can be slow, as in the European theater during World War II, or it can occur relatively quickly, as it did in Desert Storm. Both the will and the ability to fight erode, often leading to collapse and defeat.

The impact of logistics inadequacies at the operational and tactical levels is similar. Grand schemes and operational designs never get off the drawing board for want of adequate logistic support. History is filled with examples of forces missing or failing to exploit opportunities because of their inability to logisticly sustain gains resulting from success in individual battles or engagements. On the Western front in World War I, both sides repeatedly demonstrated that it was possible to penetrate the lines of defensive trenches and fortifications; what they could not do was exploit the penetrations once made, primarily due to their inability to support the advancing units.

Logistics is so important that it frequently shapes the designs of campaigns, battles, and engagements. Major operations within a campaign are frequently conducted solely for the purpose of developing the logistics capability required to sustain the campaign as a whole. The island-hopping campaign in the Pacific during World War II was largely dictated by the need to acquire advanced air and naval bases necessary to support forces striking at the Japanese homeland. Conversely, because of their importance to military effectiveness, the logistics capabilities of the adversary are often critical vulnerabilities; supply bases, lines of communications, and combat service support units are always key targets and often become the focal point for engagements and attacks.

CHARACTERISTICS OF LOGISTICS

Logistics is a complex phenomenon that defies easy explanation. Any short definition, particularly one limited to a single sentence or paragraph, will invariably fail to give a complete picture of what logistics is and what good logistics requires. Using the basic description of logistics provided above, we now examine the various characteristics of logistics.

Logistics as Science

Of all the major functions that affect the outcome of war, logistics is the most concrete. In fact, logistics has been one of the few aspects of war that has been consistently described as a science. This means that logistics benefits from a body of facts, relationships, and rules that can be put to use by those who can study and master them. These facts, relationships, and rules can form the basis for calculation, deduction, and, within the limits set by the essentially chaotic nature of war, prediction.

Because of this greater degree of regularity, logistics is an area in which extensive calculation is both possible and necessary. The number and types of ships needed to move a given force from one place to another, the fuel consumed by a unit making a road march, and the spare parts needed to support a certain fleet of vehicles can all be calculated ahead of time. The tools of the civilian engineer—standard planning factors, formulas, calculations, and rules of thumb—are thus of great use to logisticians.

This is not to say that logistics is perfectly predictable. On the contrary, anything that touches upon war, and certainly something as central to war as logistics, is greatly affected by the chaos that is at the very heart of warfare. Nonetheless, because the obstacles that must be overcome in order to move and sustain forces—time, distance, and terrain—are generally passive, the relationship between inputs and outcomes is far more regular in logistics than in tactics, operations, strategy, intelligence, or command.

Because logistics is a science, it must be thoroughly understood before it is applied. This means that the logistician must do more than pull planning factors out of a book or apply an existing template to a new situation. The logistician must think each problem through, understanding the major assumptions that underlie the calculations and the implications of any change in those assumptions. In other words, the science of logistics requires that its practitioners understand not only the various elements of logistics but the relationships between them.

Despite the strong scientific character of logistics, no single theory underlies the many activities that come under the heading of logistics. The reason is twofold. The first is the great variety of things that must be done in order to move and sustain a fighting organization. The second is that *logistics is defined less by a set of activities than by its results.* To use a simple example, the purpose of logistics is not to use a particular technique to move so many gallons of fuel or tons of ammunition, but to ensure that the fuel and ammunition are in the right place at the right time.

In contrast to the pure sciences, in which knowledge may be accumulated for its own sake, logistics exists solely for the purpose of supporting military operations. Thus, logistics is an applied science, an endeavor in which the difference between success and failure is a function not only of knowledge but of the techniques, tools, skills, and will to put that knowledge to use. Indeed, the use of logistics is so important that it makes sense to describe logistics as an art as well as a science, a critical and inseparable part of the larger art of war.

Logistics as Art

While some aspects of war fall principally in the realm of science, an even greater part of the conduct of war falls in the realm of art. Art includes the creative application of scientific knowledge through judgment, experience, and intuition to devise practical solutions. In logistics, as in all other aspects of war, it is crucial to develop a vision of what needs to be done and how to do it. In addition to technical skill, development of this vision requires creativity, insight, and the ability to recognize and assess risk. Mechanical and inflexible application of procedures and formulas can lead to paralysis and failure. Logistics must supplement analysis and calculation with foresight and intuition in order to anticipate future requirements. When circumstances change, logisticians must be flexible and ingenious in adapting to the new situation. Creativity, boldness, daring, and a willingness to innovate or even improvise when necessary are required to exercise the art of logistics. When balanced with sound judgment and decision-making skills, application of these characteristics provides the basis for successful logistics.

Logistics as Relationships

In logistics, as with any other aspect of the art of war, "the essential thing is action."[4] However refined, extensive, or accurate the science of logistics may be, it can be translated into the fact of effective logistics only if a large number of people do the right thing at the right time. Some of the actions that make up effective logistics are routine and are thus governed by preexisting rules and procedures. Other actions are ad hoc, taken in response to particular situations. The common denominator that unites these actions is their relationship to the definitive tasks of logistics, the movement and maintenance of forces. Thus, if an action helps to move or maintain a force, it is part of logistics.

The actions that comprise logistics are rarely isolated. Rather, they are but small steps in long, interrelated, and highly complex chains of activity. Originating in the civilian economy, resources pass through the levels of war and many echelons of command, connected by a network of logistics systems and processes. The intricacy of these relationships quickly becomes evident to anyone who tries fully to describe, by narrative or flowchart, all the logistic activities of even the most rudimentary military force. Nonetheless, any understanding of the logistics of a particular force depends heavily upon a good sense of the nature of these relationships.

The classic technique for making sense of these relationships is to reduce them into abstractions such as lines of communications, kinds of logistics at each level of war, and echelons of various sorts. These abstractions are simultaneously useful and dangerous. They are useful because they provide a shorthand that often captures one or more important features of a relationship—for example, its scale or geographic location. These abstractions are dangerous because they mask the inherent complexity of logistic relationships and often make them seem more straightforward than they really are.

Logistics as Organization

Because of its inherent complexity, logistics requires the sustained, creative, and systematic cooperation of large numbers of people. Such cooperation can be achieved only by means of deliberate, well-considered, and custom-tailored organization. Because of this, it is as impossible to speak of logistics without discussing logistics organizations as it is to explain modern medicine without mentioning hospitals.

The concept and details of organization for logistics can vary greatly. Factors such as geography, the national economies involved, enemy action, the organization and warfighting philosophy of the forces being moved and maintained, and the dynamics of the war being fought all play a role in determining the best logistics organization for a given force. It is even quite possible that the various activities of logistics will be carried out by a number of different organizations.[5]

The common denominator in all healthy logistics organizations is the combination of a shared vision and initiative. The shared vision, promulgated by means of a common organizational culture and the expressed views of leaders, allows the various parts of a logistics organization to set objectives, establish standards, and measure the usefulness of their work. Initiative makes it possible for all parts to solve the problems that they face and overcome the obstacles that stand in their way in a timely and effective manner.

Logistics as a Complex System

Military organizations and military evolutions are complex systems. A complex system is any system composed of multiple parts, each one of which must act individually according to its own circumstances and which, by so acting, changes the circumstances affecting all other parts. Military forces are constantly evolving, changing their size, composition, organization, and capabilities in response to the environment in which they operate. Because of this, the logistics organizations that move and maintain these forces must evolve as well. In responding to change, a healthy logistics organization functions as a complex system, operating within the complex system of the military force it supports.[6]

The most important implication of this is that a logistics organization will rarely, if ever, achieve a state where "everything goes like clockwork." Indeed, such extreme regularity is a sign that stagnation has set in and the system is probably not adapting to changing circumstances. A healthy logistics organization will thus be a work in progress with some elements in a relatively stable condition and many others in a state of flux. In times of crisis, when circumstances are changing rapidly and swift adaptation is required, logistics organizations are likely to function in nonstandard ways. Periods in which the system operates in a regular and orderly fashion will alternate with periods in which it is in considerable turmoil.

LOGISTICS AND WAR

The character of any war is shaped to a significant degree by the logistics concepts and capabilities employed to move and sustain the forces of each belligerent. At the same time, what we ask of logistics and what logistics is able to provide are profoundly influenced by the particular circumstances of a war, campaign, or battle. These circumstances include, but are not limited to, geography, climate and weather, resources, technology, population, culture, politics, style of warfare employed by forces, scale, skill of commanders, and goals pursued by the various combatants. Moreover, because all of these factors may interact with each other to produce unpredictable or undesirable results, logistics is often affected further by the dynamics of a particular battle or campaign as it evolves.

What a military force is physically able to do is limited by the way it is moved and supplied. An army supplied from bases along a single line of communications cannot execute movements, however promising they might be, if those maneuvers take it very far away from that line. The style of war employed by a military force is intimately linked to its logistics capabilities. The grand maneuvers that made Bonaparte the master of central Europe were dependent upon the Napoleonic system of drawing the bulk of needed supplies from towns, fields, and granaries in the theater of operations. When, in places like Spain and Russia, these proved inadequate, the rapid movement of large masses of men and horses so necessary to Bonaparte's success was no longer possible. The matériel-intensive style of warfare employed by armed forces of the Republic of Vietnam proved successful in the early 1970s, when the requisite mountains of supplies were provided by the United States. When these supplies were no longer available, the same style of warfare was unable to prevent a catastrophic defeat.[7]

Great feats of arms have often been made possible by the skillful exploitation of special capabilities in logistics. For his conquest of the Persian empire, Alexander the Great conditioned his troops to march with a minimum of baggage, and he developed an intelligence system that made him aware of the location of sources of food and fodder along his route of march. For the British fighting in Spain during the Napoleonic wars and the Marines who fought in the mobile phase of the Korean war, the advantage was control of the sea, which allowed operational movement and the provision of logistic support that was largely independent of traditional lines of communications. The dynamic two-division assault into Kuwait conducted by the First Marine Expeditionary Force (I MEF) during Desert Storm was made possible by the MEF's ability to create a massive forward logistic support base in the middle of the desert immediately before the beginning of the ground offensive.[8] The expeditionary logistics capabilities inherent in modern amphibious forces enabled the 24th Marine Expeditionary Unit to establish forward support bases hundreds of miles inland in Turkey and northern Iraq in support of humanitarian assistance operations during 1991.[9]

Just as logistics does much to shape the operations of war, the changing fortunes of war often have a profound effect on logistics. The winning or losing of a battle, the gain or loss of an ally, the movement of forces from one geographical area to another, and even significant changes in popular opinion and sympathies can often force radical changes in the way that a force is moved and supplied. For the first part of the

American War of Independence, the size, staying power, and operational mobility of George Washington's Continental Army was hampered by a logistics system based on an insufficient number of wagons moving on poorly maintained roads. The alliance with France brought with it the capability to supply the Continental Army by sea and thus made possible the massing and maintenance of the force that won the decisive victory at Yorktown. The capture of Seoul by United Nations' forces in the immediate aftermath of the Inchon landing in 1950 deprived the North Korean army of its logistics infrastructure and its lines of communications.[10] The deployment of the 22d Marine Expeditionary Unit to conduct noncombatant evacuation operations in Liberia during 1990 was initially envisioned as a short-duration mission. As events unfolded, the unstable security situation in Liberia required an extended commitment of amphibious forces, in turn necessitating the establishment of an extensive logistics pipeline to support the U.S. Embassy as well as the military units participating in the operation.

The Human Dimension

Though logistics deals primarily with the physical world, it has a considerable effect on the moral aspect of war. (The term moral as used here is not restricted to ethics, but pertains to those forces of a psychological rather than a tangible nature.) The moral aspect is significant because war is above all a human endeavor. War is a contest between hostile, opposing wills, a struggle in which moral factors—resolve, fear, courage, morale, leadership, will, esprit—are often more important than mental or physical ones.[11]

Logistics plays an important role in the cohesion of a fighting force. By providing the necessities of life, effective logistics frees members of that force from preoccupation with their own needs. This allows them to focus their physical and mental energies on their military duties. By providing the means of waging war, effective logistics not only gives fighters the means of dealing with the physical challenges they face but also gives them the sense of being part of a large and powerful team. By displaying economy, adaptability, fairness, flexibility, and innovation, a logistics system can foster the sense that those in charge know what they are doing. In other words, *good logistics reinforces the moral authority of leaders.*

The link between logistics and the human dimension of war can be seen during World War I in the German spring offensive of 1918. Because of the repeated failure of the German logistics system to provide adequate food and clothing to frontline troops, once German soldiers penetrated the Allied lines, many spent their time looting captured Allied supply depots. Indeed, so great was the sense of privation of many of these soldiers that they looted items that were of no immediate use to them—such as writing paper and shoe polish—simply because they had been in short supply. The immediate, physical effect of the looting was to slow down the tempo of the German attack and thus give the Allies time to bring up reinforcements and establish new defenses. More importantly, the psychological effect of the sharp contrast between Allied plenty and German shortages contributed to the widespread belief within the German forces that eventual Allied victory was inevitable.

While logistics can have a profound effect on morale and combat effectiveness, the performance of the logistics function is greatly affected by the human aspects of warfare as well. Like other military units, logistics units are composed of human beings whose capacity for action depends heavily on moral factors. Leadership, the maintenance of unit cohesion, and the provision of a clear sense of purpose are as important to the motivation and capabilities of logistics units as they are to the performance of military units of other kinds. High morale among logisticians can, by itself, no more transport supplies across an ocean than the high morale of infantrymen can, by itself, overcome the firepower of a machine gun. Nonetheless, in logistics as in other aspects of the art of war, moral limits are usually reached before absolute physical ones.

Many of the great feats of arms of military history were preceded by feats of logistics that required an extraordinary degree of courage and self-sacrifice. The 1775 siege of Boston that did so much to convert a local rebellion into the American War of Independence would not have been possible without the incredible efforts involved in transporting the artillery and supplies captured at Fort Ticonderoga during the depths of a New England winter. Two centuries later, the Vietnamese operation of 1954 to capture the French fortress of Dien Bien Phu in what was then French Indochina depended on the transport of tons of supplies by porters carrying packs and pushing bicycles along hundreds of miles of jungle-covered mountain trails.

Violence and Danger

The means of war is force, applied in the form of organized violence. Since war is a violent enterprise, danger is a fundamental characteristic of war. The actions that fall into the category of logistics are rarely, if ever, inherently violent. However, because what they do cannot be separated from war as a whole, those who practice logistics must often deal with both violence and danger. In some cases, this is the direct result of enemy action. Attacks on logistics installations and lines of communications are commonplace in modern warfare. In other cases, the danger faced by those involved in logistics is derivative, resulting from risks taken to provide needed support under conditions of bad weather, fatigue, shortages, and the sense of urgency created during combat. The famous "Red Ball Express," the logistic operation designed to supply the Allied pursuit following the breakout from the Normandy beachhead, was largely free from significant enemy interference. Nonetheless, the urgency of the operation put enormous strain on the truck drivers, mechanics, military policemen, and supply specialists who tried to make the system work. Stress, the poor quality of roads, and the tendency to push vehicles to their mechanical limits resulted in a great number of accidents and many fatalities.[12]

Because logistics is a function of war, the logistics system and the units and personnel that operate that system will be subjected to violence and danger. Commanders have an obligation to protect their logistic elements if these elements are to carry out their essential functions in support of operations. At the same time, logistic organizations must prepare for the stresses of combat. The characteristics that enable us to function in the environment of violence and danger—physical fitness, excellence in basic military skills, technical proficiency, leadership, and unit cohesion—are as important to logistic units as they are to any other type of military organization.

Friction

War is a complex enterprise subject to a multitude of factors. The interaction of these factors, the most important of which is the basic clash of opposing human wills, results in friction. In war, deliberate action of all sorts, to include logistic action, is made difficult by friction, "the force that resists all action." Activities that are a routine part of both civilian and military life in time of peace—the transportation of people and cargo, the distribution of goods, and the provision of services—become harder to carry out in war. Friction can take a number of forms. Physical friction can be caused by such things as weather, accidents, or the incompatibility of systems, equipment, or units that were not prepared to work together.

Psychological friction is the distress or disorientation that results from fear or fatigue. Both physical and psychological friction are greatly increased by enemy action.

Because it has so many causes and so takes many forms—indeed, because it is an inherent part of war—friction cannot be eliminated. It can only be reduced and overcome. A means of reducing friction is simplicity, the achievement of which requires continual efforts to eliminate needless complexity. We can overcome friction through the exercise of initiative, creativity, and will power throughout the force. Initiative greatly multiplies the number of minds and wills that take an active part in overcoming friction. Creativity increases the number of possible solutions to any given problem. Will power brings possible solutions far closer to their absolute physical limits than would otherwise be the case.

Logistics is subject to friction to the same degree as other functions in war. Logistics deals in large quantities of matériel, vast distances, and short response times; logistics employs formulas, calculations, and prediction to a greater extent than other functions. All of these actions are readily impacted upon and disrupted by unforeseen events, our own errors, or enemy action. It is important to note that logistics units, installations, facilities, and resources are not merely subject to attack but, in many cases, are the *preferred* targets of military action. We must cope with friction in logistics in the same manner as we do in other aspects of warfighting. Despite the complexity of tasks and functions in logistics, we must strive for simplicity both in the planning and execution of logistics. Designing flexibility into the logistics system provides the means for adaptation to the changes resulting from friction and for the exercise of initiative and creativity.

Uncertainty

All actions in war take place in an atmosphere of uncertainty. Uncertainty pervades battle in the form of unknowns about the enemy, about the environment, and even about the friendly situation. Because logistics deals chiefly with the physical aspect of war, we are tempted to believe that logistics is largely immune from the uncertainties of war. Logistics makes extensive use of precise calculation. Items are counted. Distances are measured. Formulas are used to predict outcomes that range from the amount of fuel a unit needs to make a road march of a given distance to the number and type of ships needed to move a given force from one point to another. Nonetheless, the uncertainty that is part and parcel of war ensures that these calculations, however necessary, will rarely be more than approximations. At times, moreover, the fortunes of war are such that the results of many calculations will bear little resemblance to reality.

We know how much a Marine needs to eat to maintain physical strength and morale, but we do not know whether a particular shipment of rations will be destroyed by enemy action or lost in an accident. We can use our knowledge to calculate the amount of food a force will need to sustain itself for a given number of days, the capacity of various transportation systems needed to move that food, and the human effort needed to turn that food into palatable meals. We cannot, however, predict with any certainty the events, such as casualties or the surrender of large numbers of enemy troops, that can greatly change the numbers of people who must be fed.

As with friction, uncertainty on the battlefield can only be reduced, not eliminated. The logistics system must be able to function effectively in an environment of uncertainty. It must not come to rely on standard formulas and calculations performed too far in advance of actual operations. The basic nature of logistics requires it to anticipate requirements based on assumptions and predictions in order to position resources where and when they may be required. Nevertheless, it is crucial that the logistics system also be able to adapt to changing circumstances, respond to new requirements, and rapidly implement alternative courses of action when initial assumptions and calculations are found to be in error.

Fluidity

For all that friction does to inhibit deliberate action, war itself is remarkably fluid. Each episode in war is the temporary result of a unique combination of circumstances, presenting a unique set of problems which require an original solution. No episode can be viewed in isolation, nonetheless. Rather, each merges with those that precede and follow it, creating a continuous, fluctuating flow of activity filled with unexpected events and fleeting opportunities.

Great advantages accrue to the military force whose logistics can adapt to changing circumstances and new situations. For this reason, logisticians must always be looking ahead, attempting to identify potential future actions and positioning logistics to support the next battle or even the battle after the next. To do this, they must have a *thorough understanding of the commander's intent* as well as an awareness not just of their own situation but the situation at the operational and sometimes even strategic levels.

The effect of fluidity and the ability of logistics to adapt can be seen in an example from the Korean war. In December of 1950, the entry of Chinese divisions into the war converted a highly successful pursuit by United Nations forces into a headlong retreat. A major factor in preventing this defeat from turning into a catastrophe was the rapidity with which the United Nations logistics system adapted to the new situation and the simultaneous inability of Chinese logistics to do the same. More precisely, logisticians of the United Nations forces were able to quickly change the means by which any given part of the force was moved and resupplied. This ensured that rear guards had sufficient ammunition, that vehicles had fuel, and that necessary improvements to routes of march—which included an entire bridge airdropped to the 1st Marine Division—could be made. The Chinese, on the other hand, remained bound to their traditional, guerrilla-style, logistics system, which assumed that combat units could draw food supplies from a compliant civilian population and that ammunition consumption would be very low. In a situation where the civilian population was either nonexistent or actively hostile and where units might be required to make several attacks in a week, this failure of the Chinese logistics system to adapt to new conditions translated directly into the failure of the Chinese forces in Korea to properly exploit significant tactical and operational opportunities.[13]

Disorder

In war, friction, uncertainty, and fluidity combine to create a great deal of disorder. Even under the most favorable circumstances, plans will go awry, orders will be misunderstood, important messages will be lost, and units will be mixed. Disorder presents particular problems for logistics, which necessarily depends on what may be called the "orderly virtues"—economy, accountability, standardization, and regularity.

Because of the great benefits that derive from a well-ordered logistics system, logisticians have sometimes made the mistake of trying to combat disorder by stubbornly enforcing procedures, even when the consequence of such enforcement is disaster. A classic example of this is the response of the British quartermasters who, at the critical moment of the battle of Ishandhlwana during the Anglo-Zulu War of 1879, insisted on issuing ammunition "by the book." Men who lacked the proper requisition forms, as well as men who requested ammunition from quartermasters serving units other than their own, were turned away. As a result, the final

Zulu charge caught many British riflemen with empty cartridge boxes and thus succeeded in overrunning the entire British position.

Not so disastrous in the short run, but nonetheless dangerous, is the belief that the disorder inherent in war is so irresistible that all considerations of economy, accountability, standardization, and regularity should be dispensed with. This belief, which was endemic to U.S. forces during the last years of World War II, resulted in such waste, confusion, and destruction that the tempo of operations was considerably slowed. Failure to properly account for supplies resulted in avoidable shortages of such things as artillery ammunition. Widespread refusal to recycle gasoline containers exacerbated already severe gasoline shortages on the front lines with consequent reductions in the ability of frontline units to exploit opportunities. Even something as simple as the littering of roads with tin cans and other garbage led to a shortage of truck tires which greatly hampered the ability of many units to make long road marches.[14]

To deal with disorder, the logistics system must strive for balance. On the one hand, it must estimate requirements and distribute resources based on plans and projections; otherwise the needed support will never be available where and when it is required. On the other, a system that blindly follows schedules and procedures rapidly loses touch with operational realities and inhibits rather than enables effective action. Logistics must balance the need for economy with the requirement for redundancy and reserve capacity. It must balance the need to anticipate with the requirement to adapt and respond. Finally, above all, it must balance the need for efficiency with the need for effective support on a battlefield characterized by friction, uncertainty, fluidity, and disorder.

LOGISTICS AND OPERATIONS

Effective logistics is absolutely necessary to the conduct of war but does not, in and of itself, guarantee victory. Rather, logistics makes an essential contribution to victory by generating and sustaining the forces that conduct military operations. In doing this, logistics enters into a tense and dynamic partnership with military operations, a relationship in which both logistics and operations exert a powerful influence on each other.

A military operation is an inherently chaotic enterprise shaped by the interplay of two or more hostile wills. It is thus necessarily dynamic. The outcomes and byproducts of battles and engagements are unpredictable. Success or failure in battle does not always bring one side or another closer to its original goal. The situation changes continuously and creates new possibilities for one or more belligerents to exploit. Because of these dynamics, the results of military operations defy calculation. The result is tension between the desire to design and implement an infinite number of creative and adaptable operational schemes and the need to operate within the realistic boundaries imposed by logistical supportability.

The relationship between logistics and military operations can therefore be stated as: *logistics sets the outward limit on what is operationally possible.* A useful analogy is that of a paddle ball, a toy consisting of a wooden paddle, a ball, and a piece of string. Logistics is like the string; it doesn't determine where the ball will go but sets a limit on how far it can go before being pulled back. Logistics provides and sustains combat power. By determining *how* it provides and sustains combat power, logistics exerts a significant influence over the design and execution of military strategy, campaigns, and tactics. By determining for *how long* it can continue to provide and sustain combat power, logistics establishes constraints for the application of this combat power.

The relationship between operations and logistics applies at all levels of war and across the range of military operations. At the strategic level, the ability of a nation to employ forces to achieve national objectives, to concentrate them in a theater of operations, to keep them there, and to have them engage in operations is directly influenced by the logistics capabilities of that nation. Russia in World War I and China during the Korean war had little difficulty raising large land armies. Concentrating them in a theater of operations and keeping them supplied once there proved far more difficult. As a result, the forces which could be employed were significantly limited; the actual combat power brought to bear was only a fraction of the country's whole capacity.

A classic example of the limitations imposed by logistics at the operational level can be seen in the series of campaigns for control of Libya during World War II. Distances were so great, the transportation infrastructure so poor, and the difficulties of moving supplies into the theater so overwhelming that otherwise successful offensives were frequently halted for lack of supplies. On the other hand, an example of logistics opening an operational window also comes from the struggle for North Africa during World War II. In the summer of 1942, Axis forces unexpectedly captured the British fortress of Tobruk. Tobruk was a major British logistics base, well-supplied with trucks, fuel, food, and ammunition. The capture of these supplies turned what had been a local offensive with limited objectives into a major threat to Allied control of the Middle East.[15]

Operations during the initial phase of Operation Restore Hope in Somalia in 1992-93 demonstrate that the limitations imposed by logistics apply to military operations other than war as well. Efforts to deliver aid to the most critically affected portions of the country were delayed by the lack of logistics infrastructure required to receive and process supplies as well as to support the military forces who would ensure the safe delivery of those supplies. Marines could not bring the relief supplies inland until the necessary support facilities were established in and around the coastal city of Mogadishu.

If logistics sets the limits, it follows that one of our key objectives must be to ensure that limits imposed by logistics do not inhibit effective operations. We do this in several ways. First, we must ensure that plans and operations always take into account logistic realities. That is, operations must not ask for the impossible or intentionally overstep boundaries set forth by logistics. Second, logistic plans must be developed in concert with operational plans. This helps ensure that logistic plans can support operational designs to the greatest extent possible. Third, logisticians must constantly strive to expand the limits of the possible by employing initiative, creativity, and adaptability in the design and conduct of logistic activities. Finally, it will often be necessary to take specific operational actions to expand logistics capabilities. Whether that means seizing a critical support facility prior to moving against an operational objective, delaying an attack in order to build up the resources necessary to exploit the results, or reducing the size of a force to help reduce the volume of support required, *commanders must consider logistics in the development of plans and the allocation of resources.*

CONCLUSION

Logistics is an integral part of warfighting. Logistic action is an essential part of military action. Logistic relationships and organization are inseparable from the web of relationships and organizations that make modern war possible. Logistics provides the resources of combat power, positions those resources in the battlespace, and sustains them throughout the execution of operations. Because it is an integral part of warfighting, logistics is subject to characteristics of war. Since war is fundamentally a human activity, it is the human dimension that is paramount in logistics. Violence and danger, moral and physical forces, friction, uncertainty, fluidity, and disorder play roles in logistics that are similar to those that they play in other aspects of warfighting. Logistics is a key component of any and every operation of war. While it does not determine the shape that operations take, it sets limits that restrict the options available to commanders. Thus, the more flexible and far-reaching the logistics, the greater the possibility for bold, decisive, and imaginative action.

Chapter 2

Logistics Theory

"A real knowledge of supply and movement factors must be the basis of every leader's plan; only then can he know how and when to take risks with those factors, and battles are won by taking risks."[1]

—Napoleon

". . . it [the description of logistics] precludes that view of logistics which sees it only as a game for the G-4s and the mathematicians—a game to be settled with loading tables, slide rules and transportation schedules.

Logistics becomes, in fact, the very core of generalship . . . to get military forces into a theater of war in superior strength and husband that strength until they shall prevail."[2]

—S. L. A. Marshall

Having reached a common understanding of the nature of logistics, we turn to an examination of the theory of logistics. This examination will provide insight into key aspects of this function that, in turn, will serve as the basis for creating effective logistics.

THE EVOLUTION OF LOGISTICS

Logistics is as old as organized warfare and, like war itself, has evolved considerably over time. Some changes, such as the introduction of new methods of transportation or new ways of obtaining supplies, have influenced logistics directly. Other changes have been indirect, the byproducts of the use of new techniques and weapons. Changes in warfare often cause momentous and unexpected changes in the conduct of the logistics function. An understanding of the evolution of logistics provides key insights into the changes and challenges facing logistics in the future.

It is possible to distinguish several general periods within the evolution of logistics.[3] Premodern armies had relatively simple logistics needs. Warriors brought their own weapons to the field and provided their own means of mobility, their own feet or a horse. The primary logistics concern was feeding the army; this was generally done through foraging or local procurement. With the emergence of modern armies in the

17th and 18th centuries came the initial development of dedicated logistics systems and services. The introduction of cannon and firearms created new requirements for supply and transportation services. The makeup of these armies and the nature of warfare during this period generally discouraged the use of foraging or pillage as a means of supplying the army. As a result, forces had to be largely self-sufficient. This led to the creation of a logistics system consisting of fixed supply points called magazines and large, unwieldy baggage trains. The logistics system required to sustain an army at once became both a key limiting factor and a major vulnerability. The need to establish magazines in advance of any campaign restricted strategic mobility, while the requirement to transport large quantities of provisions and other supplies inhibited tactical mobility. In recognition of the importance of the logistics system to these armies, attacks on magazines, baggage trains, and lines of communications became significant actions of war for the first time.[4]

The industrial revolution radically changed warfare and logistics. One of the major changes was the impact upon the scale of warfare. Weapons, ammunition, machinery, uniforms, equipment, and even foodstuffs could be produced at a greater scale than ever before. In addition, mechanization of production significantly reduced the labor requirement, freeing up manpower for service in mass conscript armies. A second major change brought on by the industrial revolution was the increase in lethality afforded by the application of new technologies in weaponry coupled with the ability to mass-produce both weapons and ammunition. Finally, developments in transportation such as the railroad and steamship and later the airplane and automobile significantly enhanced the strategic, operational, and tactical mobility of armies and their support systems. As a result of these innovations, military forces grew larger in size, could deliver unprecedented firepower, and were increasingly capable of rapid movement.

The industrial revolution transformed logistics from an important aspect of warfare to an essential prerequisite for the conduct of war. Mass armies consumed vast quantities of food, ammunition, and other supplies. Modern weapons and equipment created the need for new services such as maintenance and salvage as well as for new commodities like fuel and spare parts. The management of rail and shipping networks became crucial to delivering forces to the battlefield and sustaining those forces once they arrived. Logistics considerations came to dominate the strategic and operational levels of war. The ability of a nation to translate industrial capability into military resources and its capacity to sustain the military effort became crucial factors in determining whether to go to war. Decisions on where and when to initiate campaigns were in large part resource decisions. Major operations could not be conducted until the necessary buildup of troops and supplies had been effected by the logistics system.

The influence of these changes is clearly seen during World War II. The Japanese attack on Pearl Harbor was precipitated by the perceived threat to Japan's access to strategic resources. The Allied grand strategy of "Europe First" was based in large part on the initial inability of the logistics system to support simultaneous offensives in both theaters. Major operations such as the invasions of Normandy and the Philippines were preceded by months of logistic stockpiling.

The next major step in the evolution of logistics is only now beginning to emerge. The information age will have significant effects on all aspects of warfare, and logistics is no exception. Many of these effects will have a positive influence on logistics. The development of more capable weapons and equipment will likely result in a decrease in the size of units and a reduction in the quantity of equipment. This result should reduce the volume of logistic support needed. Modern electronics and information systems are making possible major advances in both equipment design and maintenance management. Sustainability is now considered a critical factor in the development and procurement of new weapons and systems; acquisition of efficient and maintainable equipment will also reduce the logistic burden. Improvements in information processing and communications are already permitting better management of resources than ever before. Better management in turn leads to greater responsiveness and efficiency in the provision of logistic support. The evolution of open information networks and architectures will allow the exchange of data and processes with the commercial sector, enabling us to draw upon resources and capabilities outside the military logistics system.

At the same time, the information age will also present significant new challenges for logistics. While the prevailing characteristics of the information age are variety and rapid change, we believe that the basic nature of warfare will remain much the same as it has always been: a violent collision of opposing wills driven by complexity, friction, and chance. However, the battlespace of tomorrow could be significantly different than the one we fight in today.

One of the emerging trends is the *expanding battlespace.* Improvements in mobility are permitting forces to move more quickly over longer distances than ever before. At the same time, the increasing lethality and reach of weapons enables the engagement of targets at greater ranges than ever before, compelling military units to disperse even farther in order to survive. This dispersal, in turn, creates a nonlinear array of forces with considerable separation between units and an intermixing of friendly and enemy forces to a greater extent than ever before. The battlespace of the future could also become relatively empty with much smaller forces possessing an increased destructive potential spread over greater intervals. Greater distances between combat forces and their supporting elements, as well as between the belligerents, will require our logisticians to extend their reach. Knowing how, where, and to what extent forces will be employed throughout the battlespace, anticipating and planning for their sustainment needs, and providing the mobility necessary to deliver the required support will be a considerable challenge in the extended battlespace of the future.

A second emerging trend is the *continuing compression of reaction times during operations.* Advanced weapons and information systems provide the capacity to locate the enemy, concentrate forces, and engage targets more rapidly than ever before. The notion of generating ever-increasing speed over time, or tempo, takes on greater relevance as we attempt to accelerate our information processing and decisionmaking to outpace that of our adversary's. In the battlespace of the future, operations will be spatially dispersed, but observation, decisionmaking, and reaction intervals will become shorter and shorter. Lack of time presents a particular challenge to logistics, since logistics relies in large measure upon anticipation and planning to overcome the physical constraints posed by the mass of its commodities and the distances over which they must be delivered. The resourcefulness and ingenuity of logisticians will be tested by the need to provide ever-more-responsive support to keep pace with faster operating tempos.

Another trend in future operations has been emerging for some time: the requirement for our forces to carry out *a wide variety of missions, many of which lie outside the traditional definitions of war or combat.* Forces that are primarily configured for operations in war are increasingly being required to conduct military operations other than war with little or no advance notice. Circumstances may require simultaneous execution of both types of operations or a transition from one type to the other as the nature of the military action changes. While the basic principles by which we conduct combat and military operations other than war are similar, the subtleties in application may be extensive. In efforts such as humanitarian assistance and disaster relief, logistics functions assume a preeminent role. These efforts are normally conducted as joint, multinational, and, increasingly, interagency operations. Interoperability of our logistics capabilities with those of joint forces and agencies will be critical. New and unique logistics capabilities will be required, as commanders must consider not only how to support their own forces but also those of other Services, allies, participating nongovernmental organizations, and civilian populations. Since we cannot predict the time, location, or characteristics of the next contingency operation, our logistics system must be sufficiently flexible and adaptable to function across the range of military operations, in major wars as well as military operations other than war.

A fourth trend is the *expanding use of advanced technology by military forces*. In many cases, the adoption of new technology results in the substitution of quality for quantity. The implication for logistics is that while the overall size of the inventory goes down, the value and relative importance of each individual asset goes up. The need for maintaining individual aircraft is more critical when there are 12 per squadron instead of 20. The need for effective management of assets is more apparent when there are a dozen precision-guided munitions available instead of 100 dumb bombs. The complexity of the tasks involved in supporting a high technology force also increases as the sophistication of its weapons and equipment increases.

A final trend is the *ever-increasing integration of military logistics with the commercial world.* Many logistics concepts perfected in the private sector are currently being adopted by the military and, in certain cases, major elements of our logistics capacity are under consideration for outsourcing. While efficiencies may be gained through this integration, we must also exercise some caution. We cannot forget the unique requirements imposed upon military logistics by the need to support combat operations. Consider our reliance on commercial transportation for strategic mobility. Is our own commercial air, overland, and sealift infrastructure able to respond to singularly military needs? Will an increasingly international shipping industry, where the majority of ships are no longer owned by American companies, be amenable to mobilization under tense political circumstances? What effect might this dependence have on our ability to move and sustain our forces? Logistics will have to consider these difficult questions and provide practical solutions to ensure commanders receive the support necessary to conduct and sustain operations.

The evolution of logistics provides us with the perspective from which to examine the remaining aspects of logistics theory. It shows the importance of logistics to warfare throughout history and demonstrates that the role and impact of logistics have increased over time. An understanding of the evolution of logistics also gives us some insight into the challenges facing logistics in the future.

THE LOGISTICS PROCESS

Using the evolution of logistics as a foundation, our study of logistics proceeds with a generic description of the logistics process. If logistics is the bridge which connects the resource capability of a nation's economy to its fighting forces, then the elements of the logistics process are the means by which the transition is made. The elements of the process describe how resources are used to equip, transport, and maintain our forces. The logistics process at any level consists of four steps: *acquisition, distribution, sustainment,* and *disposition.* (See figure 2, page 46.)

Acquisition is the procurement of weapons, equipment, facilities, ordnance, and commodities such as food, clothing, fuel, and repair parts. Though usually a strategic responsibility, acquisition can be accomplished at the operational and tactical levels through purchasing or securing locally available material and supplies.

Distribution is the means by which logistic support—matériel, support services, and personnel—get to the operational commander. The means employed is predicated upon *what* is being moved, its *place of origin, lift assets available*, and *urgency* assigned. Distribution is a diverse process, incorporating not only transportation means but encompassing an entire distribution system composed of bases and procedures, such as inventory control methods.

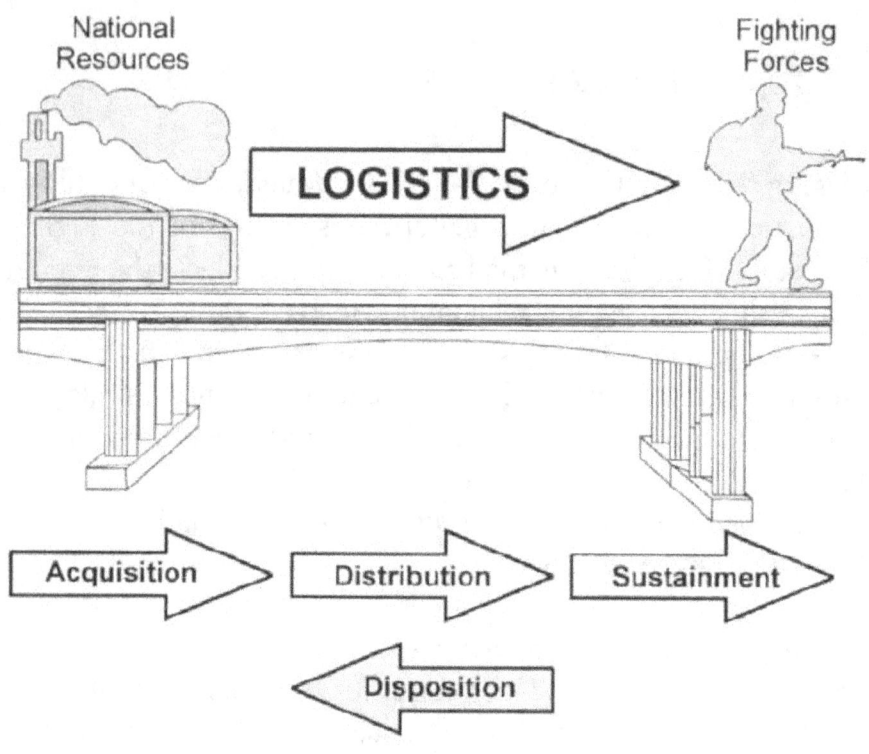

Figure 2. Logistics process.

Sustainment is the provision of resources necessary to support operations until the mission is completed. Sustainment facilitates uninterrupted operations through means of adequate logistic support. It is accomplished through supply systems, maintenance, and other services which ensure continuing support through the duration of an operation.

Disposition is the consumption and/or return and disposal of weapons, equipment, and supplies. The logistics process is complete when supplies and services are used by the supported unit or they are returned to the supporting unit for redistribution, repair, salvage, or disposal. Disposition makes a significant contribution to our ability to sustain forces over the long term and is an essential part of our fiscal and environmental responsibilities.

The logistics process provides the framework for the conduct of all logistic activities. It shapes the design of our logistics system as a whole and underpins the logistic plans generated to support specific operations. Commanders must plan for and supervise the process of acquisition, distribution, sustainment, and disposition to ensure that logistics supports, not inhibits, their operational designs.

FUNCTIONAL AREAS OF LOGISTICS

Because logistics encompasses a wide range of support activities, logistic elements are normally broken down into groupings of six related activities known as functional areas. These six functional areas are *supply, maintenance, transportation, general engineering, health services*, and *other services* which include legal, exchange, food, disbursing, postal, billeting, religious, mortuary, and morale and recreation services. Logistics systems and plans are usually developed for each functional area, and logisticians commonly discuss support concepts in terms of these "commodity areas." However, while each logistics function is essential in and of itself, all functions must be integrated into the overall logistics system to ensure full support of the operating forces. Developing maintenance plans without regard to their impact on supply and transportation is foolhardy. Health services support planning is impossible without considering supply, transportation, maintenance, and general engineering services.

LEVELS OF LOGISTICS

Logistics encompasses a wide variety of activities that serve the needs of organizations as small as a fire team and as large as a coalition of nations at war. While the logistics process and functions cut across the levels of war, the nature of logistic activities conducted at the strategic level are very different from those carried out at the tactical level. For this reason, it is important to consider levels of logistics, just as we discuss levels of war.

Levels of logistics correspond directly to the strategic, operational, and tactical levels of war. At first glance, the differences between the levels of logistics appear to be largely a matter of scale. Logistics at the strategic level of war (strategic logistics) involves greater distances and greater amounts of matériel than logistics at the operational level of war (operational logistics). Operational logistics, in turn, involves greater distances and amounts of matériel than tactical logistics. However, it is crucial to understand that the focus of logistic activities is significantly different at each of the levels of logistics. *Effective support of military evolutions depends upon the successful conduct and integration of logistic activities at all three levels.*

Strategic logistics encompasses the nation's ability to raise, deploy, and sustain operating forces in the execution of the national military strategy. It is at this level that weapons and equipment are designed and purchased, recruiting programs are initiated, and permanent bases are developed and maintained. Strategic logistics involves the management of air and sealift for strategic mobility and the sustainment of forces in distant theaters of operations. When long-term military operations are undertaken, strategic logistics requires extensive interaction with the nation's industrial base to ensure timely support of the military effort.

Strategic logistics should not be viewed as a function accomplished by someone else, somewhere else, with little or no impact on tactical logistics or the conduct of operations. Logistic investment made at this level determines the type and extent of support to the operational forces not only in numbers of personnel and quantity of food and ammunition available but also the quality, effectiveness, and supportability of the weapons and equipment we have to use.

Operational logistics addresses sustainment within a military theater of operations. It connects the logistic efforts of the strategic level with those of the tactical level. Taking resources provided from the strategic level, it makes them available in sufficient quantities to the tactical commander to support the concept of operations. Operational logistics involves those support activities required to sustain campaigns and major operations. It normally encompasses three tasks: providing resources to the tactical commanders, procuring resources not provided by strategic logistics, and managing the resources necessary to sustain the campaign in accordance with the intent of the operational-level commander.

Providing resources to the tactical commander is accomplished through the development of intermediate and forward support bases, the maintenance and employment of an effective transportation system, and support of the arrival and assembly of personnel and equipment as they reach the area of operations. Operational-level procurement involves coordination with joint support agencies, contracting for host-nation support, or even the capture and salvage of resources from the enemy. Finally, managing resources entails both the apportioning of resources among tactical forces based on the campaign plan and the rationing of resources over time to ensure sustainment throughout the duration of the campaign. Successful management of logistics at the operational level requires a thorough understanding of the commander's intent, the development of detailed and flexible logistic plans, and the maintenance of an effective command and control system.

Tactical logistics is concerned with sustaining forces in combat. It deals with the feeding, fueling, arming, and maintenance of troops and equipment. Tactical logistics involves the actual performance of the logistics functions of supply, maintenance, transportation, health services, general engineering, and other services with resources immediately or imminently available. Tactical logistics draws upon resources made available at the operational level and focuses on the provision of support within the force.

While the focus of this publication is largely on the tactical level of war, it is important to restate that successful tactical logistics is dependent upon a strategic and operational logistics foundation. *Strategic logistics forms the foundation from which operational logistics enables and sustains tactical logistics.* A logistics system must be able to transform resources provided at the strategic level into measurable and sustainable combat power at the tactical level. For this reason, it is crucial that the Marine Corps logistics system be capable of functioning at all three levels of logistics. (See figure 3, page 52.)

THE LOGISTICS SYSTEM

In order to perform the logistics function, a military organization must have a logistics system. A logistics system consists of personnel, organizations, equipment, facilities, training and

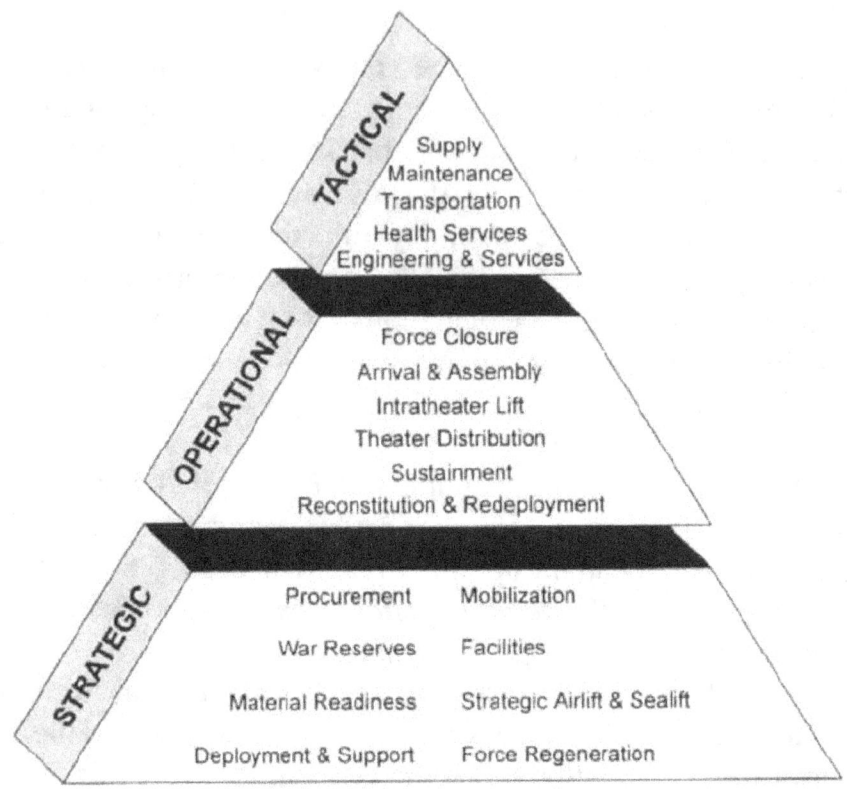

Figure 3. Levels of logistics.

education, and procedures which are integrated so as to support the operating forces. A logistics system is tailored in size, structure, and procedures to support the mission, composition, and warfighting doctrine of its military force. Before discussing the particular makeup and characteristics of the Marine Corps logistics system, it is important to develop an understanding of logistics systems in general. *All logistics systems have two fundamental elements: a distribution system, made up of bases and distribution procedures, and command and control.*

Distribution Systems

Distribution systems are made up of bases and procedures that are designed to process resources from the time they enter the military system at the strategic level until they are issued at the tactical level. In order to accomplish its objective, the logistics system must have a place from which to provide resources—*a base*—and a method—*distribution procedures*—for moving the required resources from the base to the tactical forces which need them. (See figure 4, page 54.)

Bases. Bases are an integral part of the distribution process. They form the foundation of the entire logistics system, providing the fixed points from which resources are acquired, maintained, and distributed. Bases perform several functions besides the obvious purpose of accumulating supplies for later use. Bases are a location for the provision of services, maintenance of equipment, and organization and redistribution of assets, and they often act as the transition point from one form of transport to another (such as from intertheater air or sealift to local rail or road transportation systems). Whether providing simple or diverse services, bases are the most tangible component of a distribution system. Their configuration may be as simple as the cache or as intricate as seabasing. Options available for bases include permanent bases, forward bases, seabasing, and prepositioning. (See figure 5.) The choice of a particular type of basing depends primarily on the nature of the force and the area of operations. *The expeditionary nature of the Marine Corps normally requires the employment of a combination of basing options to support a particular operation.*

Permanent Bases. Permanent bases provide sustained support for large elements of the force. They are normally established within the boundaries of the nation or a close ally where they can be fully developed and protected. Military organizations whose primary responsibility is defense of their homeland

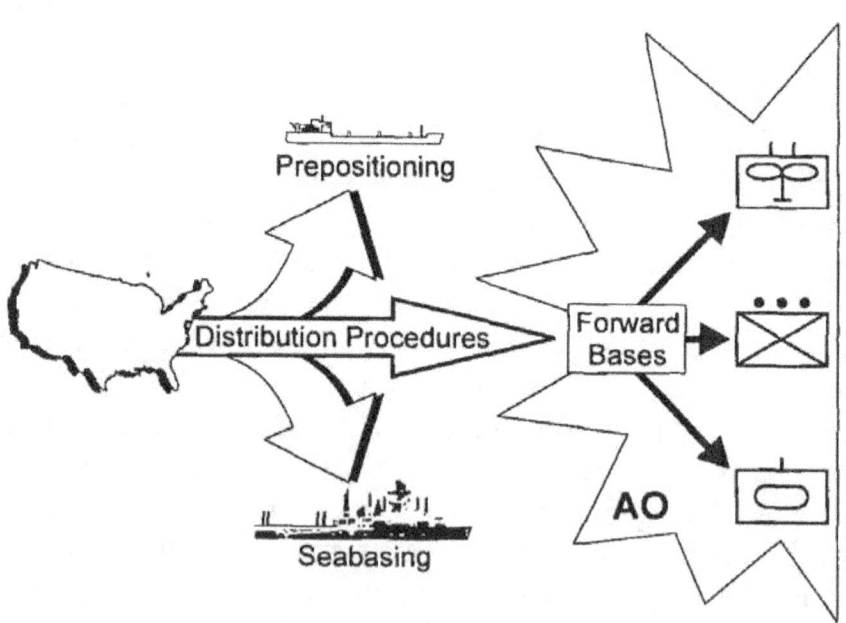

Figure 4. Distribution systems.

normally rely primarily on permanent bases to provide virtually all logistic support. In contrast, U.S. forces maintain permanent bases within the continental United States and on the soil of U.S. allies to provide strategic- and operational-level logistic support; these bases also are the core for the development of a forward-deployed operational- and tactical-level logistic support network.

Forward Bases. The classic technique for overcoming the limits that logistics places on operations is the establishment of

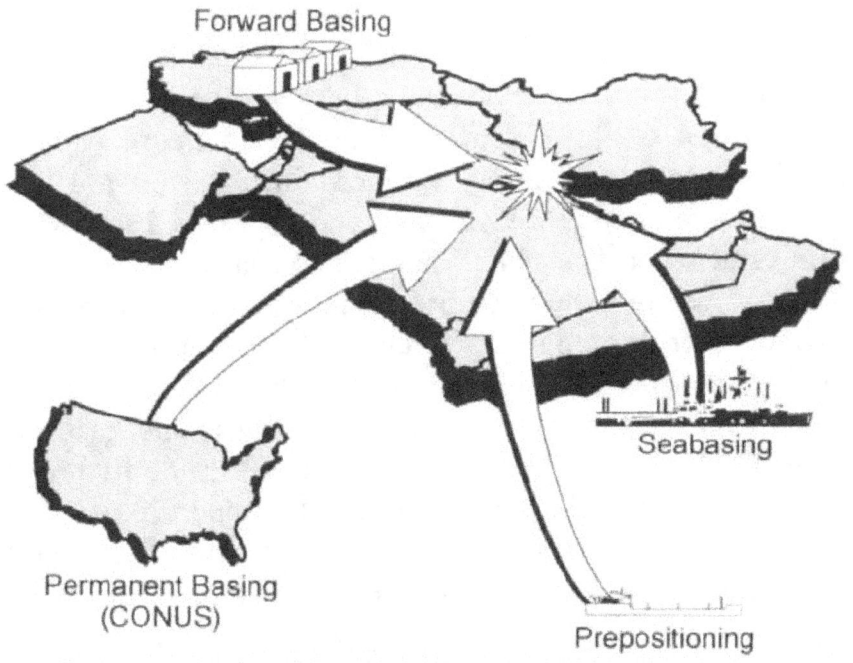

Figure 5. Logistics basing options.

forward bases. Forward bases are facilities established within the area of operations to provide operational- or tactical-level logistic support. Forward bases serve a number of purposes, the most important of which is to increase the responsiveness of the logistics system by moving the source of support as close as possible to the operating forces. Modern equipment and techniques make it possible for forward bases to provide almost every function of logistics, ranging from the performance of complex medical procedures through the overhaul of sophisticated weapons systems. Historically, almost all military forces have employed some type of forward base.

In determining where and when to establish a forward base, there is an inherent tension between the need for security and the desire to provide responsive support. Although absolute security is rarely achieved in war, forward bases should be reasonably secure from enemy action. In wars with well-established front lines, bases are usually located behind the zone where actual combat is taking place. In campaigns characterized by rapid movement, however, bases are sometimes established at times and places where their chief protection is the tempo of operations. Such was the case with Forward Operating Base Cobra established inside Iraq by the U.S. Army's 101st Airborne Division to support initial air assault operations during Operation Desert Storm.[5] The better protected a base is, the greater the odds that the people working there can focus their energies on the logistic effort.

However, the advantages gained by providing a highly secure environment must be weighed against the considerable benefits that come from locating bases as close as possible to the actual fighting. These benefits include the efficiency of transport and the speed with which the logistics system responds to the needs of the front.

A classic use of forward basing was illustrated by Grant's 1864 campaign against Richmond. In order to increase the mobility of his marching columns, Grant reduced the rations carried by his soldiers from eight days to three. Each corps was stripped to march with only about one-half its usual supplies. Supplies were restocked from advance depots which had been staged along established rail and water routes. The result was a series of forward bases, positioned far enough ahead along Grant's route of march to support his movement south to Richmond.[6]

Seabasing. Ships and boats have been used as forward bases in riverine operations, amphibious operations, and operations in the littoral areas. Seabased logistics is the managed provision of sustainment to units ashore from ships offshore. The advantages of this approach can be considerable. During the invasion of Okinawa in 1945, a 6,000-mile maritime supply line was used to support an invasion force of over 400 amphibious ships and almost 200,000 troops.[7] In the disaster relief effort conducted by the 5th Marine Expeditionary Brigade after a typhoon devastated Bangladesh in 1991, Navy and Marine units provided significant assistance to the host nation without the need to establish a presence ashore or draw resources from the already overburdened local infrastructure.[8] Ships can serve both as a means of moving supplies into a theater of operations and as mobile warehouses for resupply within that theater. Certain kinds of ships can provide useful facilities, to include small hospitals, maintenance capabilities, freshwater condensers, living quarters, and galleys. Seabasing reduces the need to establish logistics facilities ashore, thereby reducing the footprint and vulnerability of the land-based portion of the force.

Seabasing is not without its drawbacks. The chief prerequisite to the use of ships as forward bases is friendly control of the surrounding water. If a forward base on land is properly laid out, it takes considerable enemy action to destroy it. A ship at sea, on the other hand, can be sunk by a single torpedo, antiship missile, or mine. The most recent example of this took place in the Falklands war of 1982, where a British ship serving both as an improvised aircraft carrier and as a depot for aviation supplies was sunk by a single Exocet missile.[9] The movement of support between the seabase and shore is critical and must receive proper priority in the allocation of transportation assets. If ship-to-shore transportation assets are limited, the need to move combat forces may conflict with the need to move logistics resources ashore.

In the past, seabasing was appropriate only under limited circumstances. While it provided for greater economy, it often resulted in a loss of responsiveness due to time/distance factors, difficulties in communications, and the effects of weather on ship-to-shore movement. Generally it provided little more logistics capability than supply, hospital assets, and limited maintenance facilities. Today, however, advances in amphibious shipping, aircraft, landing craft, and communications and information systems are rapidly improving the ability to perform seabased logistics. A seabased logistics system which employs these capabilities will often be able to provide logistic support with equal or greater flexibility and responsiveness than could be provided from forward land bases. This enhanced capability, coupled with the increasing requirement to reduce the dependence of our forces on all types of land bases, will result in greater emphasis on seabasing in the future.

Prepositioning. Prepositioning is a variation of forward basing. Prepositioning is the staging of equipment and supplies in a forward location for use by a force at some future time. One of the oldest and simplest forms of prepositioning is the cache, the technique of concealing a small quantity of supplies in a hidden location for later use. Today, military forces use prepositioning as a means of decreasing the time it takes to respond to a crisis by reducing the need to transport large quantities of supplies and equipment to the area of operations. Large countries preposition equipment near their borders for use by units or reserves stationed in the interior. Nations with commitments to an alliance may preposition stocks on the territory of their allies both as a sign of commitment as well as a means to increase responsiveness.

U.S. military forces in general and the Marine Corps in particular make extensive use of prepositioning. Forward-positioned equipment and supplies are intended to bridge the gap between the time a force's initial supplies run out and the time that strategic resources begin to flow into the theater of operations. Prepositioned stocks may be stored ashore at permanent bases on the territory of allies or aboard military or commercial shipping. Included in these prepositioning programs are weapons and equipment to outfit combat formations, supplies, repair parts, and the transportation, medical, and maintenance equipment needed to provide basic sustainment to a deployed force.

The flexibility and responsiveness which prepositioning offers are illustrated by the employment of maritime prepositioning ships in support of recent operations. During the initial days of Operation Desert Shield, a Marine air-ground task force (MAGTF) of over 15,000 Marines was deployed a distance of 12,000 miles to link up with prepositioned equipment and supplies on board the ships of Maritime Prepositioning Squadron Two. Within 11 days, the 7th Marine Expeditionary Brigade was fully combat-capable, providing the first heavy forces for the defense of Saudi Arabia. The resources of the prepositioning ships were used to sustain the MAGTF as well as the forces of other Services and allies while full logistics capabilities were being established in theater. Maritime prepositioning ships have also demonstrated their utility in supporting military operations other than war, providing support to humanitarian assistance operations in Somalia and disaster relief efforts in the Philippines.

We must consider a number of factors to determine which basing options to employ within a logistics system. The most important of these factors is the basic mission of the military force. A continental power will use a different type of basing scheme than a maritime power. A force primarily organized for territorial defense will place much less emphasis on forward basing or seabasing than military forces structured for expeditionary operations.

The second major factor is security. Bases must be protected. Protection is normally afforded by locating bases at safe distances from direct combat or by allocating sufficient forces for base defense. Permanent bases located deep in the rear area are generally more secure than forward bases, but the responsiveness of the support provided is also often greatly reduced. Employing forward bases in close proximity to the front increases responsiveness, but significant forces may be needed to defend these bases; forces used in base defense cannot be used for other operations. Seabasing offers increased security in many situations but at a potential cost of some degree of responsiveness.

The final factor is tempo. As a general rule, it takes far longer to amass supplies or establish maintenance resources at a base than it does to expend or use them. An extreme example is provided by the Gulf War. In that conflict, coalition forces spent 6 months accumulating supplies at forward bases but exhausted many items of supply in less than 100 hours of combat. Because it is far easier to expend supplies and services than to accrue them, the maintenance of a high operational tempo will often depend on the speed with which forward bases can be established. This requires the investment of resources: having adequate goods and services, sufficient means to transport them to the forward base, and skilled logisticians who can effectively manage those assets. The choice of a basing scheme can influence tempo. For example, prepositioning can generate tempo by reducing the demand on strategic transportation assets. At the same time, prepositioning can inhibit tempo if the equipment and supplies are not prepositioned at the right locations.

As a forward-deployed, expeditionary force-in-readiness, the Marine Corps employs a combination of basing methods. We use permanent bases to carry out strategic logistics functions and to support the development of forward-deployed operational- and tactical-level logistics capabilities. As a naval force, the Marine Corps has always made extensive use of seabasing. The Navy-Marine Corps team has pioneered innovation in the conduct of logistics functions afloat. Examples include modern hospital ships, the aviation logistic support ship, and the offshore petroleum distribution system. Seabasing will become even more critical in the future since the characteristics of future operating environments will require greater security for forces ashore and less reliance on developed infrastructure within the area of operations. At the same time, seabasing will become more attractive as emerging technologies increase our capabilities to do seabased logistics. Prepositioning has become an essential part of our logistics concept, allowing us to increase responsiveness and generate tempo at the strategic and operational levels. Finally, the Marine Corps uses forward basing once forces are established ashore. Some of these expeditionary bases are collocated with a beach, port, or airfield where they provide the necessary links to seabased resources. Others are positioned close to the front in order to provide responsive support to the operating forces.

Procedures. To provide logistics resources to the forces from the bases just described, the other major component of a distribution system is a set of procedures. Reduced to its simplest form, there are two types of procedures that can be employed to effect distribution. The first places almost total responsibility on the unit needing support. When a unit requires support of some type, it generates a request. The logistics system provides resources from the bases in response to the request. This type of procedure is known as "demand-pull" or simply "pull." At the other extreme, it is possible to design a system that provides resources without any action on the part of the unit receiving support. Resources are delivered to the base and automatically allocated among the units supported by that base according to planned schedules and formulas. This method is referred to as "supply-push" or simply "push."

The push concept uses calculations of anticipated logistics requirements to position or deliver resources where and when they are likely to be needed. While normally associated with supply, the push concept can be applied to most logistics functions. Medical facilities can be prepositioned based on projected casualty rates in certain sectors. Maintenance teams can be moved forward in anticipation of future requirements. Push logistics develops detailed plans for the provision of support and provides resources on some type of schedule. The push concept relieves the tactical commander of much of the burden to project logistics requirements and request the support; it provides regular and generally dependable support. On the other hand, because push logistics relies on anticipation and planning, the tactical commander may be overburdened by excess quantities of certain items while going short in others. The push concept requires accurate estimates for the tempo of operations and corresponding consumption rates. Underestimating results in shortages while overestimating results in unnecessary resources spread throughout the area of operations. In addition, pure push systems usually lack the flexibility to respond to the dynamic needs of combat.

In the pull method, the operating unit directly controls the orders for resupply as well as calls for engineering, maintenance, and other support services. The supported unit takes on greater responsibility for anticipating and defining requirements as well as ensuring that those requirements are submitted in time to arrive where and when required. The advantage is that the tactical commander receives only the support that is actually needed. This permits forces to enhance their mobility by carrying the minimum quantities of supplies or support assets. The benefit to the logistics system is greater efficiency through the reduction in the overall quantity of resources required. While pull systems may be more efficient, their effectiveness depends on the logistics system's ability to successfully react to the extensive requirements that may be placed upon it. The success of the pull technique has greatly improved with enhanced communications and information management, as well as a more responsive distribution network. However, there will always be limits to the ability of any system to react to the uncertainties of war.

In war, consumption rates can be unpredictable, communications between the operating forces and the support infrastructure may be limited or unavailable, and delivery times may be uncertain. The dilemma for the commander is whether to rely on "push" support based on anticipated needs or on "pull" support as determined by user demand. *Marine logistics traditionally employs a combination of both methods.* (See figure 6.) Initial sustainment is provided by the push method; strategic and operational agencies push most of the projected logistic support into the area of operations based on the anticipated level of operations. Tactical units receive routine support, such as resupply of food, water, and ammunition, on a standard schedule based on their consumption rates and employment. At the same time, units pull specific kinds

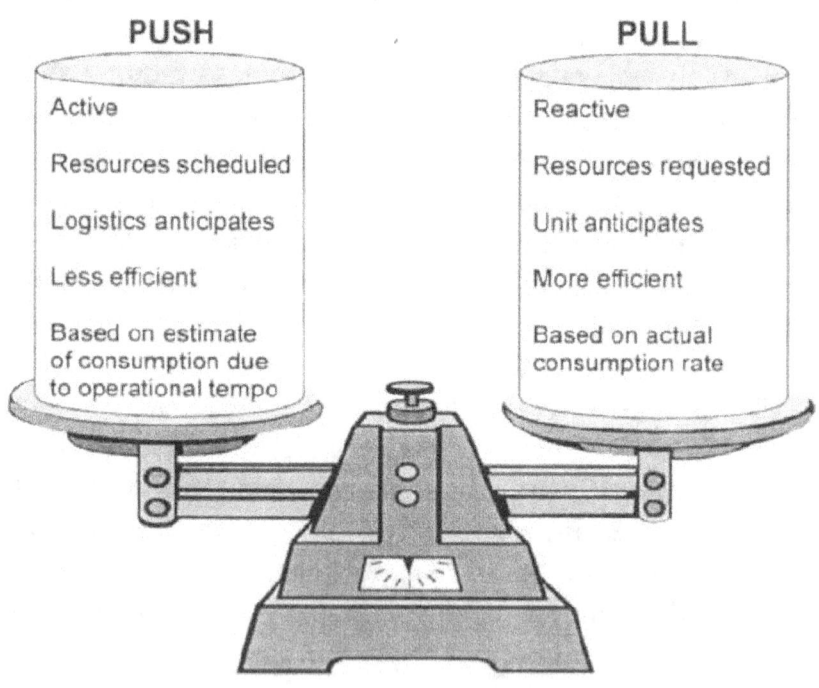

PUSH

Active

Resources scheduled

Logistics anticipates

Less efficient

Based on estimate of consumption due to operational tempo

PULL

Reactive

Resources requested

Unit anticipates

More efficient

Based on actual consumption rate

Figure 6. Push versus pull distribution.

of logistic support, such as maintenance, engineering, and medical services, from task-organized combat service support units or detachments on an as-required basis.

A related aspect of distribution procedures is the method used to actually deliver the resources to the supported unit. There are two principal distribution methods. In *supply point distribution*, resources are staged at a base or other point and the supported unit comes to that base or point to obtain its supplies or services. The using unit is responsible for transportation to and from the supply point. The other method is *unit distribution.* In this method, the logistics system delivers supplies and services directly to the supported unit. The supporting logistics unit provides transportation to the supported unit.

Supply point distribution is more efficient for the logistics system but places a greater burden on the supported units. Unit distribution is generally more responsive to the needs of the operating forces but requires the dedication of significant transportation assets. While certain situations might require the use of one method over the other, the two distribution methods are normally used together to effect the delivery of resources.

Command and Control

The second component of the logistics system is command and control. The best distribution system in the world is useless without an effective means for using that system to take the necessary actions. Command and control is fundamental to all military activities.[10] Command and control is the means by which a commander recognizes what needs to be done and sees to it that appropriate actions are taken. In logistics, command and control helps the commander to recognize what support is needed and to see to it that the support reaches the units who need it.

Command and control of logistics capabilities links the distribution system to the planning and execution of operations. A critical task of logistics is to *facilitate the effective use of limited resources* to support operations. Command and control is the means to ensure this effective employment of resources. Logistics command and control aids the commander in accomplishing three essential tasks: anticipating future requirements, allocating resources, and dealing with uncertainty.

Planning is the component of command and control that provides the primary means of anticipating future requirements. Planning is crucial to all military activities, but it is essential to the effective conduct of logistics, given the quantity and variety of resources to be provided, the diverse nature of the logistics requirements to be satisfied, and the impact of time-distance factors on the provision of timely support. Logistics must stay one battle ahead of operations in order to support the commander's intent and help shape the battle or campaign. Effective logistic planning identifies future requirements and designs solutions to satisfy those requirements. Logistic planning ensures that the necessary resources can reach the area of operations through *force deployment planning* and that all operations can be adequately supported through *sustainment planning*.

Logistic planning benefits from the scientific nature of logistics. Since logistics deals in quantifiable resources and tangible factors, analytical methods, formulas, and calculations can help to develop logistic plans. In this respect, logistics has taken advantage of the increasing availability of modern communications and information systems. Information technology has enhanced the collection of usage data, the tracking of assets, and the processing of requirements, providing more detailed and accurate information upon which to base plans. At the same time, we recognize that there are limits to what can be quantified and that logistic plans and calculations are only as reliable as the operational assumptions upon which they are based.

While planning can aid us in anticipating requirements, we recognize that even the best supported forces will suffer shortages of supplies and services. This may be the result of poor planning, enemy action, an unanticipated shift in the character of an operation, or simply an unforeseen change in the fortunes of war. Whatever the cause for the shortage, command and control must provide the means for allocating limited resources in accordance with the requirements of the situation. Most logistics systems employ a system of priorities to help resolve this dilemma.

Priorities constitute the relative order of need for a commodity or service.[11] Priorities may be assigned based upon the particular mission or tasks assigned. For example, the unit carrying out the most critical task often receives first priority for support. Sometimes the importance of a resource to a unit's continued effectiveness may determine priority. In this scheme, units with the most urgent need for supplies or services in order to keep operating will have first call on those resources. Distributors of virtually all commodities and services employ some type of priority system. The use of priorities is most critical in the allocation of combat-essential or life-sustaining resources such as ammunition or medical support. Priorities for the distribution of scarce resources can also depend on the pattern of battles and engagements as well as what is happening in the overall campaign. *The establishment of priorities and the allocation of resources in accordance with those priorities is a function of command, not logistics. Command and control implements the priorities determined by the commander.*

The value of establishing priorities in logistics was illustrated in the Korean war. After the Chinese entry into the war, the 1st Marine Division was surrounded near the Chosin Reservoir in northern Korea. The division needed significant supplies to fight its way out, but overland supply routes were cut off. Resupply of troops in the reservoir area became the first priority for the Combat Cargo Command of the Far East. A massive aerial resupply effort followed, providing the division with the ammunition, food, fuel, and other supplies it needed to conduct a breakout.[12]

We recognize that uncertainty is an inherent characteristic of war and that it will be impossible to anticipate and plan for all future requirements. Logisticians spend much of their time dealing with unanticipated demands. For this reason, logisticians must develop considerable expertise in solving a great variety of problems. *The command and control procedures, organizations, and support structure that aid logisticians in their work must provide flexible tools that aid, rather than hinder, rapid and responsive problem solving.*

Because the stakes of war are so high, the cost of failure so great, and the needs of comrades-in-arms so urgent, logisticians will often be tempted to focus all of their energies on dealing the with unanticipated demands on an ad hoc basis. In many cases, this will be appropriate. In others, there will be a pattern to these demands that suggests a change in approach that leads to a solution to the problem. In the fighting around Metz in the fall of 1944, for example, American logisticians were overwhelmed with emergency requests for 60mm mortar ammunition. As the U.S. supply system was, at that time, stretched to its breaking point, logisticians decided that the way to deal with these requests was to fabricate mortars that could fire the supplies of 50mm mortar rounds that had recently been captured from the enemy.[13]

EFFECTIVENESS VERSUS EFFICIENCY

Successful logistics requires both effectiveness and efficiency. While we would like to obtain total effectiveness and complete efficiency in our logistics system, we must usually accept a degree of inefficiency to ensure effectiveness or must sacrifice some measure of effectiveness in order to achieve greater efficiency. This reality creates an inherent tension, as we attempt to find the proper balance between effectiveness and efficiency.[14]

If we had unlimited resources, we could devote all our attention to effectiveness. We could provide each unit with supplies and services not just for its immediate needs but for any possible future needs. Distribution would be based on a push system and would use the unit distribution method of delivery, relieving the supported unit of most logistics responsibilities. Planning factors would include generous safety margins to ensure resources were always available. Command and control would be highly decentralized with each unit having its own full-service logistics organization and capability.

We must be careful, however, not to equate the effectiveness of logistics simply with the quantity of goods and services which are provided. Providing too many supplies can be as disruptive as not having enough. Consider the use of margins for error. While it may seem that we should include margins for error in all our calculations, this practice can significantly reduce the overall effectiveness of the logistics system and degrade the quality of support it provides. Margins for error translate directly into the need to procure additional items, increased inventory at many points in the distribution chain, and increased strain on storage and transportation. Supplies that are superfluous are just as expensive to buy and just as ponderous to move, store, distribute, and account for as necessary stocks. Service requirements that were overestimated can result in overabundance at one point and deficiencies at another.

Rather than attempt to provide "a little extra, just in case," we must strive to make accurate requirements forecasts and be prepared to adapt and innovate when those forecasts fall short of the mark or when weather, enemy action, or some unforeseen circumstance renders those predictions obsolete. As the situation changes, our logistics system must have the flexibility and responsiveness to make the required alterations in the chain of production, transportation, and distribution.

On the other hand, if the objective is simply to maximize efficiency in our logistics system, we would probably use a pure pull system, filling requirements only in response to a specific request. We would rely primarily on supply point distribution, minimizing the burden on the logistics system to deliver supplies and services. Logistic planning would continuously refine formulas and calculations in an effort to achieve increasing precision in predicting requirements and allocating resources. We would attempt to reduce the amount of resources on hand to the lowest possible level, providing little or no safety margin to deal with unforeseen occurrences. Command and control would be highly centralized in an effort to ensure positive control of all assets at all times.

In an effort to improve efficiency, military logistics is attempting to apply logistics techniques developed in the commercial sector where "just-in-time" inventory management and improved methods for forecasting demand are well established. We should not hesitate to employ any technique which offers a means to increase our capabilities. However, in considering the adoption of these techniques for military purposes, logisticians can never forget that their objective and the environment in which they operate differs significantly from that of their business counterparts. Business is focused on the provision of a product or service in a safe and cooperative environment.[15] Methods that prove efficient in peacetime will not necessarily succeed under the far more demanding conditions of war. For example, the ability of a parcel service to deliver a package anywhere in the world in a matter of hours is based on the assumption that no one is shooting at the aircraft carrying that package.

The essential lesson of this discussion is that we must balance effectiveness and efficiency in the conduct of logistics. Efficiency contributes to effectiveness. While we always need to consider efficiency in our logistics system, effectiveness in the support of operations takes precedence over efficiency. Logistics must consider not just efficiency and cost-effectiveness, but operational readiness and the requirement to deliver support in an environment characterized by violence, danger, friction, uncertainty, fluidity, and disorder. We must sacrifice some measure of efficiency to maintain effectiveness. Furthermore, we must ensure that *efficiency does not become an end unto itself. Effectiveness should always be the defining feature of our logistics system.*

APPROACHES TO LOGISTICS

Having studied the evolution, process, functions, and levels of logistics, as well as the elements of logistics systems, we conclude with an examination of approaches to logistics. We can place approaches to logistics on a spectrum according to their degree of independence. At one end of the spectrum is complete dependence on outside sources for support. Military units which have no organic support capabilities draw all sustainment from the local surroundings. Ancient armies that lived by foraging used this approach, as do certain modern guerrilla groups. At the other end of the spectrum is total self-sufficiency. The force brings with it everything it needs to sustain its efforts. (See figure 7, page 76.) While no force achieves complete independence from use of local resources, 18th century European armies, colonial armies in the 19th century, and modern naval forces most closely approximate self-sufficient forces.

Figure 7. Approaches to logistics.

A military force's approach to logistics must be tailored to its own warfighting philosophy or strategy. Around the world, the vast majority of military units are designed to fight within their own countries or on the territory of an immediate neighbor. Forces organized for territorial or home defense generally have limited logistics organizations. They do not expect to fight far from their permanent bases and can draw on local sources for basic supplies. Conventional armies and air forces have extensive support requirements. While they normally have organic logistics organizations to satisfy unique military requirements for ammunition and maintenance, most armies and air forces, even those configured for forward deployment, rely heavily on local procurement for basic commodities such as water, food, fuel, or construction material.

In contrast, forces developed to conduct expeditionary operations tend to be more self-sufficient. Expeditionary forces are often explicitly designed, trained, and equipped for overseas service. Their organization and equipment emphasize economy, flexibility, and deployability. Expeditionary forces often operate in areas where resources or infrastructure are limited. Many universal items like fresh water, lumber, or even sand are not reliably available in these parts of the world. Consequently, an expeditionary force must be prepared to carry, have delivered from a permanent base, or fabricate every single item it needs. Naval forces configured for expeditionary operations are the most self-sufficient. They are capable of conducting operations independent of support from permanent or forward land bases for an extended period. They are self-reliant, self-sustaining, and adaptable to the most austere environments.

In practice, most military organizations use a mix of organic capabilities and locally procured resources to sustain their operations. The Marine Corps, however, is a naval force designed for expeditionary operations. *The nature of the operations we conduct and the environments in which we operate demand an approach to logistics that emphasizes self-sufficiency.*

CONCLUSION

We have examined a variety of theoretical aspects of logistics. The evolution of logistics demonstrates that warfare and logistics are inextricably linked; changes in warfare can have a profound impact on logistics while changes in logistics capabilities can in turn alter significant components of warfare.

The evolution of logistics also shows that the relative importance of logistics as a function of warfare has been steadily increasing. The logistics process provides a framework around which to build a logistics system. The discussion of the functions and levels of logistics illustrates the scope, complexity, and interrelationships of logistics and demonstrates that a logistics system must be capable of carrying out all six functions and operating at all three levels of logistics in order to fully support the operating forces. In examining the makeup of any logistics system, we identified bases, distribution procedures, and command and control as key elements. We noted that Marine forces must make use of a variety of basing options, a combination of push and pull distribution procedures, and flexible and responsive command and control. Finally, we compared approaches to logistics, ranging from complete self-sufficiency to total dependence. We concluded that expeditionary warfare requires the Marine Corps to provide forces that are largely self-sufficient. In the next chapter, we discuss the features of a Marine logistics system based on the characteristics described above.

Chapter 3

Creating Effective Logistics

"When Marines go ashore, they start from zero. Pioneering logistics troops . . . build sustainability ashore to support operations across the entire spectrum of combat with the entire range of logistics. Combat logistics is second nature to Marine logisticians. . . . All this translates to an innate responsiveness and relative ease of movement."[1]

—C. E. Mundy, Jr.

"The way to meet . . . logistical demands is to flow your resources to the focus of effort—the highest priority need at the time. This requires flexibility, in the form of intelligent, well-trained Marines . . . ."[2]

—J. A. Brabham

Acknowledging the basic nature and theory of logistics outlined in the first and second chapters, we can now discuss how to make logistics work for us. What are the characteristics of effective logistics, and how can we best incorporate them into our force?

THE CHALLENGE TO LOGISTICS

Let us review some of the challenges facing logistics. What obstacles must our logistics system overcome, and what must it accomplish? First, *logistics must enhance, not inhibit, our operational designs.* While we know that logistics establishes the limits of what is operationally possible, we must build a logistics system that *extends those limits* as far as possible. Second, *our logistics system must anticipate requirements,* positioning support in advance of stated needs in order to facilitate tempo and enabling us to fight the present battle, the next battle, and the battle after next. Next, since we recognize that friction and uncertainty will make it impossible to anticipate all requirements, *our logistics system must be flexible, adaptable, and responsive.* It must be able to respond to unanticipated demand and rapidly shift support to exploit opportunities as they arise in the battlespace. Finally, *our logistics must be effective yet efficient.* It is important that our logistics system does not have overstocks and inefficiencies that drain our combat power. At the same time, we must ensure we do not sacrifice combat effectiveness for the sake of efficiency.

We must accept some measure of inefficiency in order to provide the margin of safety required to deal with unforeseen circumstances. Said another way, we must guard against logistics becoming an end unto itself, and ensure that logistics is always focused on the support of operations.

MANEUVER WARFARE

Our logistics capabilities must first and foremost support our warfighting philosophy. Marines are guided by the philosophy of maneuver warfare, an approach to warfighting that emphasizes rapid, focused effort, tactical and operational flexibility, and decentralized adaptation.[3] Because this approach is primarily concerned with the enemy, and particularly the destruction of the enemy's cohesion, it is easy to think that maneuver warfare has little to do with logistics. This is not true. The practice of maneuver warfare has fundamental implications on the way a force is organized, moved, managed, and supplied. All Marines must understand how logistics influences the conduct of maneuver warfare. While logistics units normally do not directly attack the enemy, their actions have a significant impact on the ability to gain an advantage over the enemy, generate tempo, and exploit opportunities. If Marine forces are to execute maneuver warfare, logistics units and logisticians who move and maintain those forces must not only be able to support maneuver warfare but must also apply its precepts to their own actions.

Centers of Gravity and Critical Vulnerabilities

Maneuver warfare focuses on the enemy. The aim is to present the enemy with a series of dilemmas in which events happen unexpectedly and more quickly than the enemy can react to. Marines attempt to identify the adversary's *centers of gravity*, those elements from which the enemy draws strength, and to locate *critical vulnerabilities* which, if exploited, can help us destroy, neutralize, or undermine the centers of gravity. Our logistics capabilities must allow us to seek out and exploit these critical vulnerabilities. Logistics must provide us the flexibility to avoid attacking an enemy's strength and the agility to exploit opportunities and to strike at known weaknesses. It must expand, not restrict, our operational possibilities. At the same time, we must ensure that our logistics capability does not become a critical vulnerability that our foe can exploit. We must protect our logistics bases and units while building redundancy into our logistics system, preventing the enemy from disrupting our efforts simply by striking at our logistics.

Focus of Effort and the Main Effort

Identification of the enemy's centers of gravity and critical vulnerabilities helps us to concentrate our efforts on objectives most likely to achieve success. The enemy elements on which we will concentrate are the *focus of effort*. The unit or task organization which will perform the key actions against this target is the *main effort*. Identifying the focus of effort and designating a main effort to concentrate on the focus of effort are the commander's bid to achieve a decision. The commander ensures that all forces support the main effort either directly or indirectly.

Like our combat and combat support capabilities, our logistics capabilities must be focused. As a rule, the main effort is first in line for most resources. It is at the main effort that a given resource is most likely to have the greatest impact on the outcome of the battle or campaign. This does not mean, however, that the main effort should be burdened with resources that it does not need. Providing too much or the wrong kind of resources can hinder the main effort as much as a lack of support. Neither does it imply that we should consider only the needs of the main effort. We cannot support the main effort at the exclusion of all others. All essential activities require some degree of support, even if that support is limited to basic life support such as food, water, and medical assistance. Likewise, the inclination in favor of the main effort excludes resources or activities that cannot have a timely effect on the battle or campaign. Nonetheless, in the absence of a compelling reason to the contrary, the main effort should have the highest priority for scarce supplies and services.

All units contribute to the provision of logistic support to the main effort, not just logistics organizations. Units not at the main effort can enhance its logistic support by reducing to the lowest possible level their use of resources that are useful to the main effort. These resources include supplies, the services of logistics units, and the attention of those responsible for the overall logistic effort.

We also recognize that opportunities in the battlespace are fleeting and that the enemy will try to protect critical vulnerabilities. As the situation changes, the commander may designate a new main effort or even change the focus of effort. *Our logistics system must provide the flexibility and agility that enable us to exploit opportunities as they present themselves.* It must be able to anticipate developments and position resources to support future requirements, in effect staying one phase ahead of the current battle. At the same time, the logistics system must adapt to unforeseen circumstances and be able to shift the logistic focus in concert with any shift in the main effort.

Tempo

Maneuver warfare depends heavily upon the use of tempo, both as a means of exploiting opportunities and as a weapon in its own right. Tempo is the consistent ability to act fast, to sustain rapidity of action over time. We seek to operate at a higher relative tempo than the enemy. Superior tempo allows us to seize the initiative and dictate the terms of combat, forcing the enemy to react to us. *Logistics makes a critical contribution to the generation and maintenance of tempo.* An effective logistics system enables us to quickly focus combat power and sustains that combat power throughout the course of operations. Logistics can maintain tempo by rapidly delivering supplies, repositioning forces, and repairing or replacing damaged equipment. Finally, a responsive logistics capability enhances tempo by anticipating requirements and adapting to new requirements, expanding rather than limiting the commander's operational possibilities.

Maintaining tempo requires that logisticians be extraordinarily alert. Logisticians at all levels must be aware of the full scope of the operation so that, at any given time and place, they understand what needs to be done to keep it moving forward. They must exercise considerable initiative, doing what needs to be done as soon as it needs to be done. Supporting tempo requires logistics units to operate at a high tempo. In high-tempo operations, displacements are often rapid and frequent, facilities are usually austere, and priorities may shift frequently. Greater demands will be placed on junior leaders and individual Marines, who will have to possess a wide range of technical, military, and leadership skills. While the techniques used to provide services at times resemble the classic assembly line, there will be no room for the assembly line mentality. Overspecialization, in which a person is trained to do a small number of highly repetitive tasks and then insulated from other duties, is rarely compatible with a high tempo of operations.

In seeking to support a high tempo of operations, we must be careful not to mistake haste for energy, confuse sloppiness with boldness, or substitute activity for action. Maintaining a high tempo of operations requires deliberate action tailored to the needs of the moment, not self-generated friction. A logistics unit operating at a high tempo may not seem busier than a similar organization operating at a slower tempo. However, each action performed by members of the unit operating at high tempo is more likely to be a purposeful one and less likely to be a matter of habit or routine. That is to say, every member of a logistics unit operating at a high tempo must constantly ask, "What is the best way for me to use my limited time and resources to help my supported unit fulfill its mission?"

Commander's Intent

If logisticians are to support a high tempo of operations, they cannot waste time waiting to be told what is required of them. Rather, they must make a concerted effort to understand what the commander is trying to do and the commander's plans for doing it. The commander's intent describes the purpose of the assigned task. A clear understanding of the intent becomes the basis for unity of effort and the exercise of initiative. Like all other participants in an operation, logisticians must internalize the commander's intent to the point where it becomes the common property of the entire force. This shared understanding allows logisticians to make informed judgments about such things as the allocation of resources, the best techniques for moving units and supplies, and the best approach to providing various services.

The value of the commander's intent can be seen in all sorts of operations but is most obvious in situations where formal communications break down. One of the immediate effects of the German offensive that began in March 1918 was the psychological paralysis of the command structure of the British Expeditionary Force. While this breakdown precluded the issuance of coherent orders for a number of days, it did not hinder logistics units from effectively participating in the defense. Thanks to a shared understanding of the defensive battle developed during a series of discussions held the previous winter, British logisticians were able to make the best use of remaining resources to support the deployment of provisional combat units and operational reserves. These forces eventually brought the attack to a standstill.[4]

MARINE LOGISTICS

Logistics is a Service responsibility.[5] Therefore, it is essential to support the Marine Corps' warfighting philosophy with Marine-style logistics. The Marine logistics system is designed to meet the particular demands of naval expeditionary operations and the peculiar needs of high-tempo, fluid, and decisive operations required by our warfighting philosophy. Marine logistics provides the unique capabilities which make Marine forces rapidly deployable, self-reliant, and self-sustaining.

Expeditionary operations project combat power over great distances. Forces must be able to deploy far from their home bases and fight effectively when they arrive. An expeditionary force's value lies in its ability to reach a distant area of operations in a timely manner, project power at the required time and place, and sustain the effort until the mission is accomplished. The conduct of expeditionary operations from the sea places additional demands on the expeditionary force. The force must be largely independent of land bases and capable of responding to a wide variety of missions on short notice. Naval expeditionary operations require an approach to logistics that emphasizes self-sufficiency and capabilities tailored to function in the littoral environment. This has specific implications for the force as a whole and the logistics system in particular.

Marine forces must be designed for expeditionary operations. We must build our forces with *deployment* and *sustainment* in mind. Our organization and equipment has to be efficient as well as effective. While our forces must have the required capabilities, we must always remain conscious of our limited transportation assets. Aircraft seats, boat spaces, and cargo capacity are valuable commodities which must be used wisely. Units, weapons, and equipment that can perform multiple functions and provide significant capabilities in a variety of missions are more useful than assets which are specialized for the conduct of a single function or mission. We must consider sustainment requirements in addition to operational capabilities in designing our force; capabilities which

cannot be maintained or supplied are useless in an expeditionary environment. Doctrine, procedures, and training and education must emphasize discipline in the use of resources and
the ability to adapt basic capabilities to meet the requirements
of many different scenarios.

Marine logistics must be able to build logistics capabilities
where no capabilities exist. Our logistics must provide the
self-sufficiency required to execute naval expeditionary operations. It must be able to create or deliver all of the supplies
and services required to sustain the force. It must be able to
function in austere environments without reliance on permanent bases or a developed infrastructure. Our logistics system
must be *naval in character*, capable of operating with equal
agility on land, at sea, or in the littoral region where the two
environments meet. It must be able to exploit the advantages
inherent in naval operations through the seabasing of logistics
and maritime prepositioning. At the same time, it must be
able to freely and rapidly transfer resources from ship to
shore, ensuring continuous support of forces ashore. While
our logistics capability must be largely self-sufficient, we
must possess the infrastructure and interoperability to draw
from national, theater, or host-nation logistics resources when
we conduct extended operations ashore.

Like the forces it supports, our logistics capability must be
flexible and *economical*. It must have the flexibility to support

the variety of missions our forces will be called upon to execute. It must provide this flexibility without pausing to reconfigure or deploy additional assets. The logistics system must not take up more space or consume more resources than are absolutely necessary. We cannot afford to sacrifice combat power in order to carry excess capacity.

An additional characteristic of naval expeditionary forces is the ability to "*recock*." Our forces can complete one mission, reembark, and move on to the next task without hesitation. Our logistics system must contribute to this capability. Our logistics system must have the *agility* and *redundancy* to do more than one thing at a time. It must be able to shift its focus and adapt to rapid changes in the course of a campaign or major operation. We must consider redeployment as well as deployment in designing our capabilities and ensure that we can depart with the same urgency as we arrived. Generating combat power is not sufficient; we must also place an emphasis on regenerating that combat power once it has been expended.

Core Capabilities

Logistics must be tailored to the conditions under which a military force operates. To provide the forces necessary for expeditionary warfare, the Marine Corps must possess certain *core logistics capabilities*. These core capabilities cut across the three levels of logistics and encompass all six logistics functions.

In order to generate, deploy, and sustain expeditionary forces, the Marine Corps must have strategic-level core logistics capabilities which enable us to procure weapons and equipment, mobilize forces, prepare and stage units for deployment, regenerate forces, and effectively manage the flow of resources from the strategic to the tactical level. *Strategic-level core logistics capabilities are embodied in an acquisition system, bases and stations, facilities required for the maintenance of unique Marine equipment and the provision of Service-specific supply items, and effective Service-level command and control of logistics.*

If the Marine Corps is to fulfill its role as a fighting force for regional contingencies, it must possess operational-level core logistics capabilities to support force closure, sustainment, and reconstitution and redeployment of Marine forces in theater. *Operational-level core logistics capabilities include the establishment of intermediate and forward support bases, the ability to support the arrival and assembly areas for troops reaching the theater, the ability to coordinate with joint, other Service, and host nation agencies for provision of continued support, the capability to reconstitute and redeploy forces for follow-on missions, and operational-level command and control for the effective planning and management of operational-level logistic efforts.*

If the Marine Corps is to practice maneuver warfare within the littoral regions of the world, it must have tactical-level core logistics capabilities which can deliver flexible and responsive combat service support to meet the needs of the forces engaged in operations. *Tactical-level core logistics capabilities required are supply and maintenance systems to provide matériel readiness, transportation systems to effect distribution, services, general engineering, health services, and tactical-level command and control which links operation plans and the resulting logistic requirements to logistic capabilities and responses.*

Planning

Successful logistics begins with planning. The objective of Marine logistic planning is to match the deployment and sustainment activities of our logistics system to the logistic requirements of the operating forces. Planning provides the means to evaluate the feasibility of various tactical options and to determine the adequacy of resources to support them. It assists us in anticipating requirements and positioning resources to meet those requirements. It establishes the framework for the execution and coordination of logistic support in accordance with the commander's intent and the concept of operations. Planning also provides the basis for adapting to new situations; through their participation in the planning process, logisticians gain situational awareness, facilitating their ability to deliver flexible and responsive support when confronted with changing circumstances.

Logistic planning encompasses all three levels of planning: conceptual, functional, and detailed.[6] (See figure 8.) Conceptual planning establishes overall objectives and develops broad concepts for action. *Logisticians must participate in the commander's conceptual planning* to ensure that operational concepts under consideration can be supported by the resources available and that logistic factors have been taken into account in the development of the operational design. Participation in conceptual planning also provides the logistics planner with the understanding needed to develop functional and detailed logistic plans that can support the operation plans.

Functional planning involves the development of general plans for the conduct of specific warfighting functions such as aviation, fire support, intelligence, or logistics. Logistic functional plans establish the overall logistic support concept and lay out the framework for the development of detailed plans for specific logistics functions. Because of our expeditionary nature, Marine *logistic functional planning at the strategic and operational levels usually encompasses two related planning areas: force deployment planning and sustainment planning.* Both are critical to the development and maintenance of combat power within the area of operations. *Force deployment and sustainment plans must be developed concurrently to ensure that the required combat elements can be deployed and sustained to accomplish the mission.* At the tactical level, logistic functional planning develops the concept of combat service support.

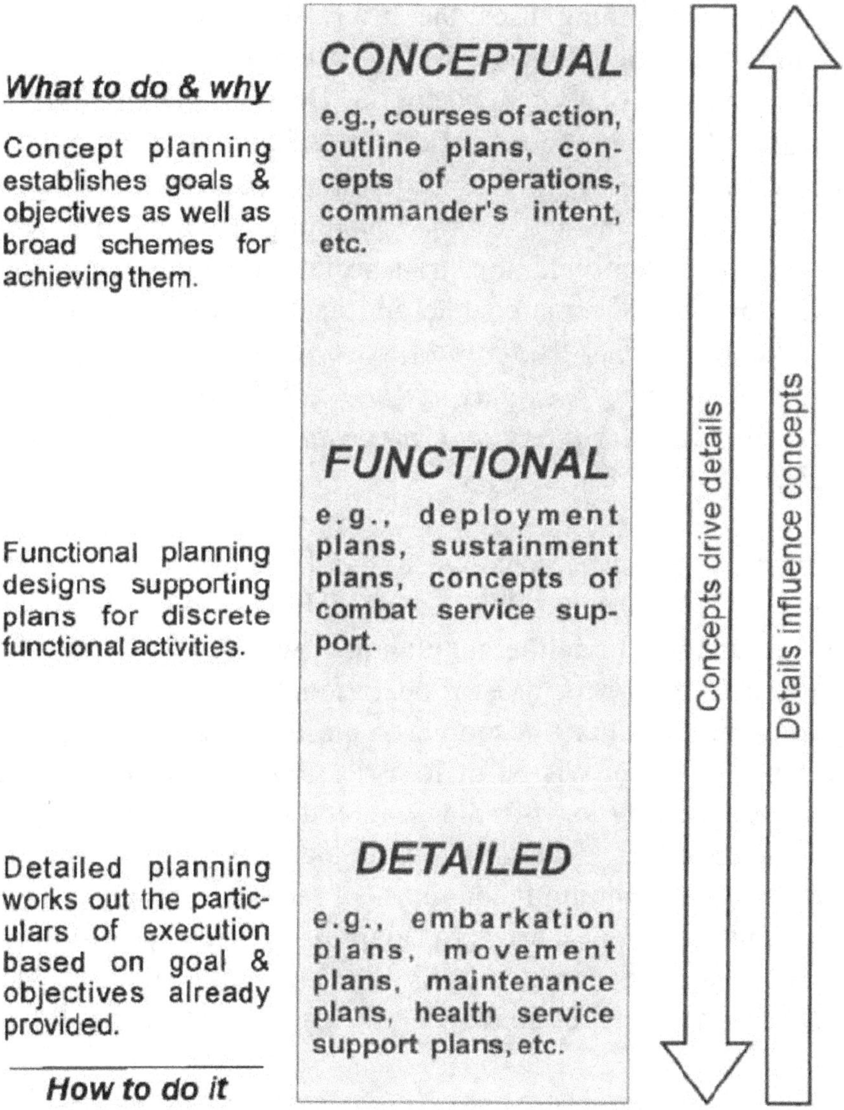

What to do & why

Concept planning establishes goals & objectives as well as broad schemes for achieving them.

Functional planning designs supporting plans for discrete functional activities.

Detailed planning works out the particulars of execution based on goal & objectives already provided.

How to do it

CONCEPTUAL

e.g., courses of action, outline plans, concepts of operations, commander's intent, etc.

FUNCTIONAL

e.g., deployment plans, sustainment plans, concepts of combat service support.

DETAILED

e.g., embarkation plans, movement plans, maintenance plans, health service support plans, etc.

Concepts drive details

Details influence concepts

Figure 8. Levels of planning.

95

Detailed planning uses the broad designs of conceptual planning and the framework of functional planning to make comprehensive plans for execution. Detailed planning works out the scheduling, coordination, or technical issues involved with directing, moving, and sustaining forces. Much of logistic planning is, in fact, detailed planning. Detailed plans are developed for embarkation, transportation, supply and resupply, provision of maintenance and health services, and other logistics functions. It is important to remember that *effective detailed planning depends on the establishment of sound functional logistic plans and integration with the conceptual plan for the operation.*

Planners must be sensitive to the time available. Logisticians must be able to plan in both deliberate and rapid planning situations. In deliberate planning, we use time to develop our knowledge of the area of operations, analyze potential requirements, calculate resources required, detail a number of options for the provision of logistic support, and test and refine the resulting logistic plans. In addition to developing the plans themselves, during deliberate planning, we practice and improve our planning techniques. In rapid planning, we meet the requirements of a crisis by adapting an existing plan to the current conditions or by rapidly developing a new plan which provides the basis for supporting the operational concept.

We strive for three primary characteristics in the development of logistic plans: integration with operation plans, flexibility, and simplicity. If our logistic plans are to expand the limits of our operations, they must, first and foremost, be integrated with operation plans. It is incumbent on the commander to ensure that the concept of operations is logisticly supportable in every phase of execution. Integration is achieved in part by designating a main effort and providing a clear statement of intent around which all aspects of the operation are planned. It is also achieved by ensuring that the planning process is participatory, involving the commander and all members of the staff. Participatory planning means cooperation both horizontally and vertically within the organization; logistics planners must be intimately familiar with the details of intelligence, operations, fire support, and aviation plans just as representatives of those functions must participate in the development of logistic plans. Finally, integration is aided by the development of mutual understanding and implicit communications among the commander, the logistician, and the rest of the staff during training evolutions.

Logistic plans must be flexible in order to deal with the uncertainties of war and adapt to changing conditions in the battlespace. Flexible logistic plans support the execution of a variety of different operational courses of action. These plans may even have specific branches and sequels to the basic logistic plan so that we can anticipate requirements related to the course of future operations. We build flexibility into our logistic plans by providing a number of ways to provide support so that minor oversights, shortfalls, or unforeseen circumstances will not undermine our efforts.

Finally, our logistic plans must be as simple as the situation allows. Providing logistic support to Marine forces operating in an expeditionary environment is an inherently complex task. Logisticians must develop plans that rapidly deploy large forces over vast distances and that sustain those forces by providing huge quantities of resources and a wide variety of services while engaging in high-tempo operations on land, in the air, and at sea. Logistics planners employ complex tools such as usage data, consumption rates, personnel and equipment densities, asset tracking systems, and other data bases and information systems in an effort to calculate requirements and match resources to those requirements. *While the problem facing the logistician is complex and the methods used to develop a solution may be sophisticated, this does not necessarily mean that the resulting plan must also be complicated.* A good logistic plan recognizes that in warfare the simple becomes difficult and the difficult seemingly impossible. We build our logistic plans around simple, compelling concepts. We ensure that the underlying intent behind the concept is understood, reducing the requirement for detailed and explicit instructions covering every eventuality. We attempt to limit the number of actions required in the plan to the minimum. We rely on methods and standing operating procedures developed and perfected during training to reduce the complexity of specific logistics processes.

Command and Control

Planning makes up an essential and significant part of command and control. Planning provides the means to anticipate future requirements and, through preparation, to adapt to them prior to execution. We must also be able to adapt to situations as they unfold. Command and control of logistics capabilities provides the means for implementing our logistic plans and for modifying those plans based upon unfolding events. Effective command and control of logistics helps to anticipate demand, enables the tailoring of resources to specific needs, and provides responsiveness to the requirements of the operating forces. A commander's ability to control the logistics system and adapt to changing circumstances can have a significant effect on the flexibility and momentum of operations.[7]

Logistics must make the most effective use of limited assets in order to generate and sustain combat power. *Command and control of logistics helps ensure the effective employment of resources in the face of competing demands raised by forces engaged in operations.* Logistics command and control enables us to monitor unfolding events, make sound and timely decisions on resource allocation, and implement those decisions quickly, facilitating the generation and maintenance of tempo.

Because of inherent tension between the limited availability of resources and the widespread need for those resources, logistics generally requires greater centralization of control than other military functions. Centralized control helps make most efficient use of resources in environments where operating forces are competing for limited assets. In addition, centralized control provides the commander with the flexibility to allocate critical resources based on changing conditions or in response to new opportunities. At the same time, we recognize that centralization can inhibit responsiveness, initiative, and the ability of individual units to exploit opportunities. Thus, we seek to achieve a balance in the degree of control used by our logistics system. In general, we employ greater centralized control at the strategic and operational levels of logistics and attempt to decentralize the performance of tactical logistics functions to the maximum extent possible.

BUILDING CAPABILITIES

An effective logistics capability is made up of many components. Organization, personnel, doctrine, education and training, procedures, and equipment all contribute to the development of a responsive logistics system. *The most important element in any logistics system is the people who make it work. Marines are the key to the execution of effective Marine logistics.* More than anything else, it is the people, those who are supported by the logistics system and those who provide the support, who determine whether it will succeed or fail, whether it supports the decisive maneuver of friendly forces or aids the enemy by contributing to friction. For this reason, we will discuss the human factors critical in building an effective logistics capability—leadership, discipline, attention to detail, and responsiveness—before turning our attention to the other key aspects of our logistics system.

Leadership

Like all endeavors in war, effective logistics depends upon leadership. *Logistics is a command responsibility, not the exclusive province of technicians or specialists.* Commanders must lead the logistic effort, just as they lead all other aspects of their command. They do this in several ways. They provide a clear statement of intent and the specific guidance required to focus the logistic effort. They ensure that logistics considerations are integrated throughout the planning process, that operation plans are supportable, and that the logistic plans which will generate and sustain the unit's combat power are developed in conjunction with those operation plans. They supervise the logistic effort, amplifying and clarifying guidance when necessary and lending the commander's influence where required to ensure the unit receives the necessary support from outside agencies. Finally, the commander supports the efforts of logisticians, ensuring that they are an integral part of the team and encouraging their exercise of boldness and initiative while carrying out the commander's intent.

During operations, logistics sections and units must perform complex tasks under difficult and dangerous conditions. Aggressive and enthusiastic leadership from officers and noncommissioned officers is required to ensure effective performance. Just as in combat or combat support units, leadership in logistics units strives to build teamwork, mutual trust, and a willingness to exercise initiative. Said another way, *effective leadership is the key to effective logistics.*

Discipline

Discipline is another critical factor in providing effective logistics. Discipline is required because demand will almost always exceed available resources. Requests for unneeded resources clog the system and block the distribution of needed material. Demands for excess support—that little extra "just in case"—can place an extraordinary burden on the logistics system; when repeated across an entire force, these demands create what has been called the "snowball effect," an ever-increasing requirement for unnecessary resources which reduces both effectiveness and efficiency. Overstating the urgency of a request for support undercuts the system and results in the diversion of resources from the main effort.[8]

A logistics system enforces discipline through the establishment and administration of priorities and allocations. Nevertheless, no set of procedures will be effective without the commitment of the people who use and operate the system to make it work. Discipline starts with the commander.

The commander of a unit must set the standards and enforce discipline within it. Discipline must also extend throughout the organization. In war, as in most other human endeavors, the most important form of discipline is self-discipline. Self-discipline makes it possible for individuals to subordinate their personal needs, desires, and interests to the greater good of their unit, their Service, and their country. More specifically, self-discipline enables a hungry Marine to distribute rations fairly, a tired Marine to doublecheck the details of a requisition, and a scared Marine to go into harm's way to make a repair or deliver ammunition.

Attention to Detail

Logistics is a highly complex enterprise in which no simple theories or easily learned management techniques can substitute for detailed knowledge of a wide variety of subjects. Logistics involves dealing with, among other things, people, money, equipment, ammunition, fuel, food, water, ships, aircraft, roads, ports, and medical services. Each of these, moreover, has a logic of its own. For this reason, a logistician must be a master of detail. The logistician must be able to understand, in all its complexity, the reality represented by a long list of items or the abstract codes on a computer printout. The logistician must be able to see patterns that arise from raw data, establish the relationships between small problems, and discover the root causes of big ones. In solving these problems, the logistician must use the full powers of a Marine leader to devise and implement systematic solutions. In most cases, these will involve alterations to existing procedures and, usually more important, a mixture of training and education that alerts other Marines to a problem and empowers them to deal with it.

Responsiveness

Responsiveness is often the yardstick by which effective logistics is measured. Stated simply, responsiveness is the ability to provide the right support, at the right time, at the right place. *It is through responsiveness that we build confidence in our logistics system.* A responsive logistics system makes logistics a force multiplier; a nonresponsive logistics system is an anchor holding back the efforts of the entire organization. It is in responsiveness that the real alliance between logistics and operations is either established or dissolved. For this reason, responsiveness is an essential characteristic of logistics.

Planning, procedures, information systems, and other parts of the logistics system help develop responsiveness in the system, but it is *the attitude and skills of the people who operate the system that determine whether it will be responsive.* Logisticians understand that war stimulates requirements which cannot be predicted through usage rates or maintenance schedules. Not only are logisticians responsible for identifying and providing the tangible, quantifiable elements of making war, but also through their service they provide reassurance and peace-of-mind that the needs of the force will always be met.

If they are to anticipate requirements and provide responsive support, logisticians must possess a broad operational perspective, superior technical skills, initiative, flexibility, and a notable sense of innovation. Logisticians must thoroughly understand the commander's intent and concept of operations in order to formulate the functional and detailed logistic plans. They must have a thorough knowledge of tactics and operational art and understand how the commander thinks—factors which do not always maximize the potential for logistic efficiency.[9] Knowledge of the plan and commander's intent facilitates the anticipation of requirements. Situational awareness and tactical experience alert the logistician to the possibilities of what might happen in the fluid battlespace. This is not a new concept. In an April 6, 1864, letter to the Commissary General, General William T. Sherman described the ideal commissary officer as one who "would converse with me freely, learn my plans, the strength of my various columns, routes of march, nature of supplies, and everything, and who could direct the harmonious working of the whole machine."[10] Moreover, "the logistics officer needs to position himself far enough forward to stay abreast of the tactical situation and react quickly to changing operational demands as he sees them developing. Being an efficient order-taker is not enough."[11] To be responsive, logistics must be flexible enough to accommodate the ebb and flow of operations. We must develop and nurture our logisticians to ensure they have the necessary skills to make this happen.

Doctrine

Doctrine represents the fundamental teachings of our profession. It establishes the way we practice our profession, providing the basis for harmonious action and mutual understanding. All Marine Corps doctrine is based on maneuver warfare. As discussed earlier, all our logistics capabilities are designed to enable us to carry out the philosophy of maneuver warfare. Likewise, logistics doctrine is derived from our doctrine of maneuver warfare. As developed in this publication, *logistics doctrine requires the execution of logistics in a manner which allows us to seek and exploit opportunities, to expand, not restrict, our operational possibilities, to develop a concept of logistic support in accordance with the commander's intent and the focus of effort, and to help generate and sustain a high tempo of operations.* This logistics doctrine establishes a common perspective for the conduct of the logistics function throughout the Marine Corps. It forms the foundation for the development of detailed tactics, techniques, and procedures for the execution of various logistics processes. Finally, logistics doctrine provides the basis for education and training in logistics.

Education

Professional military education is a continuous, progressive process of development. As leaders progresses, they come to understand the techniques and procedures of their particular military specialties and the interrelationships between different fields in the Marine Corps. Because logistics is an integral and inseparable part of warfare, *all Marines* must develop a sound understanding of the importance of logistics, the interrelationship of logistics and operations, the characteristics of our logistics capabilities, and the functioning of the logistics system. Marines must be educated in the capabilities and limitations of logistics, know how the logistics system works, and learn the procedures and techniques for requesting and receiving support. Most importantly, *they must understand how and why logistics sets the limits on operations and what they must do to ensure effective support for their units.*

Likewise, the professional education of the logistician cannot focus merely on the techniques and procedures of the logistics system; it must begin with the study of the larger art of war. Before logisticians can judge the soundness of a particular approach to operational logistics, they must understand the design of the campaign. Before they can determine the utility of a particular technique for combat service support, they must understand the character of the supported force. Thus, the traditional means of studying the art of war as a whole, particularly the study of military history, theory, organization, technology, and geography, as well as the playing of war games, are as useful to logisticians as they are to any other military professionals. Building upon their knowledge of the larger art of war, logisticians need to develop particular insight into logistics itself. Resources available for this include studies of the role played by logistics in particular campaigns, war games in which players are required to consider logistic factors and make decisions about logistics, and the technical literature dealing with all of those things—from transportation infrastructure to information technology—that have an impact on logistics.

Training

Training is the key to combat effectiveness. An effective logistics capability is developed through continuous, progressive, and challenging training. All Marines must be trained to carry out their personal logistics responsibilities from the maintenance of individual weapons and equipment through the exercise of proper logistics discipline. Marines in the logistics specialties must master the techniques pertinent to their particular occupational field. Combat and combat support units must practice logistic procedures in conjunction with their regular training. Logistics units must conduct unit and collective training, developing teamwork while mastering the tactics and techniques required to provide effective support. Integrated training among logistics units and the units they support is essential. Integrated training builds an appreciation for each other's capabilities, limitations, and requirements while providing the opportunity to develop and refine support concepts and procedures. Finally, it is critical that training prepare Marines to function effectively in the environment of combat. *Logistics capabilities must be stressed and tested in a realistic manner during training exercises.* Exercises which use garrison resources or methods to provide logistic support do not provide effective training for logistics units and create a false sense of security in the minds of supported commanders.

Procedures

While logistics as a whole, or even the support of a specific unit, cannot be reduced to a pattern, there is much to be gained by the use of standard procedures. Procedures assist in our effective conduct of logistic operations by helping to overcome friction and guiding actions in an environment of uncertainty. Well-designed and properly employed, standard procedures can simplify routine tasks and thus greatly increase the efficiency with which certain duties are fulfilled. They can also help impose discipline in the logistics process. Finally, standard procedures can help integrate logistics capabilities across the three levels of logistics and among the various agencies that participate in the logistics process. The closer the resemblance between the forms, practices, and procedures used within the Marine Corps and those of the outside world, the easier it will be for Marines to coordinate with outside agencies, businesses, facilities, and equipment.

Standard procedures are, however, a double-edged sword. Poorly designed or improperly employed, standard procedures can deprive logisticians of the power to act. *Our use of logistic procedures is always guided by the commander's intent and the priorities which result from the application of that intent or other commander's guidance.* Those who use a procedure must be able to understand its purpose as well as the methodology behind what they are doing. This understanding not only increases the chances that the procedure will be used properly but also reduces the temptation to work around the system when there is no need to. In addition, a procedure whose purpose and function are well understood is less likely to be used in circumstances where it does more harm than good.

Our logistic procedures should be designed for simplicity and speed. They should be designed for simplicity so that we can master them easily and perform them quickly under conditions of uncertainty and stress. They should be designed for speed so that we can generate tempo.

Organization

The Marine Corps employs a basic organization for the conduct of operations, the MAGTF. Every MAGTF has an inherent combat service support capability. However, the specific combat service support capabilities resident in a particular MAGTF will be tailored to the anticipated requirements of the MAGTF's mission. Thus, Marine logistics organizations reflect the central requirements of all Marine organizations: deployability and the flexibility to task-organize. *In developing the logistics organization appropriate to a particular situation, we attempt to ensure unity of effort, effective command and control, efficiency in the employment of resources, responsiveness to the supported units, and flexibility to adapt to changing circumstances.*

In peacetime, the organization of most logistics units is based on a particular logistics function: supply, maintenance, motor transport, medical, and engineering battalions are examples. This type of organization provides efficiency in the delivery of services in response to a wide variety of garrison, contingency, or training and exercise requirements. For operations, our logistics organization usually combines a number of functional capabilities into a single unit. Task-organized combat service support elements or detachments provide logistics capabilities tailored to the anticipated requirements of specific operational units.

This organizational concept helps provide commanders with the support they need while using limited logistic resources effectively and efficiently to carry out the overall operational design. However, implementing this type of organizational concept presents a different challenge than employing a single, standard logistics organization. Commanders of logistics units must be able to provide manned, trained, and equipped components of their units capable of operating independently from the parent organization. Logistics personnel must be flexible and creative in their ability to tailor their organizations and equipment for a variety of missions and environments. Finally, they must thoroughly understand their own capabilities as well as how their capabilities complement those of other logistics units in supporting the overall operation in order to rapidly create an effective, integrated combat service support element.

The flexibility and capability inherent in Marine logistics organizations was demonstrated during Operation Desert Storm. To support the 92,000 Marines participating in Desert

Storm, the Marine Corps deployed two full force service support groups made up of almost 14,000 Marines and Sailors. The 1st Force Service Support Group primarily carried out general support logistics functions for the entire Marine expeditionary force. It was organized largely along functional lines and ensured the receipt of services from the ports and airfields and their delivery to the major tactical formations.[12] The 2d Force Service Support Group provided direct support to the combat forces. It was organized into a number of task-organized combat service support detachments. The capabilities of each of these detachments were tailored to the needs of the supported operational unit and appropriate elements of the combat service support detachment were designed to accompany the supported unit as it advanced into Kuwait. The result was a fully integrated logistics organization which provided the full range of logistic support from the arrival of resources in theater through the delivery of specific supplies or services to units engaged in tactical evolutions.

Equipment and Technology

Equipment used by the Marine Corps must be supportable. *In developing new weapons or systems, logistics considerations should be balanced with performance characteristics to reduce rather than increase logistics requirements whenever possible.* To meet the requirements of a force-in-readiness, our equipment must be deployable by our strategic, operational, and tactical transportation systems. To function in the expeditionary environment, our equipment should be efficient to operate and easy to maintain. We should pursue standardization to ease the problems of interoperability and increase the efficiency of the logistics systems. Standardization, however, is not an end in itself. The case of the officer who prevented Union acquisition of repeating rifles during the American Civil War illustrates the limits of standardization. In this case, the desire to preserve a single standard for rifle ammunition prevented the acquisition of a weapon that would have had a revolutionary impact on the battlefield. Finally, in procuring weapons and equipment, we must take a long-term approach; we must buy not only the individual weapons or systems but the maintenance capabilities, parts, and training required to keep the equipment operational throughout its life cycle.

Like other Marines, logisticians make use of a great deal of equipment. Like other military equipment, that used by logisticians should be simple, robust, and adaptable. In addition, because of the close connection between logistics and the civilian worlds of commerce and industry, equipment used in military logistics often has to be compatible with existing standards of size, weight, data transmission, voltage, and the like. This leads to a strong prejudice in favor of using off-the-shelf rather than custom-designed equipment for the performance of logistics functions.

Technology is becoming increasingly important in the execution of all military functions. *We employ technology in logistics to enhance the performance of our logistics personnel.*

In this way, logistics information systems act as a force multiplier in the battlespace. They enhance logistic planning and execution by helping to process support requests, track resources, store consumption rates and usage data, estimate future requirements, develop schedules, and monitor the progress of ongoing activities. Logistics information systems contribute to situational awareness by exchanging detailed information among various logistic elements as well as among logistics, operations, and plans sections. These systems also aid in communicating decisions concerning the allocation, distribution, and movement of assets. We use technology to automate routine functions and improve the flow and value of information within the system. At the same time, we realize that technology is a tool to assist us; technology does not provide the understanding and judgment required to operate an effective logistics system.

Conclusion

Logistics is an integral and inseparable part of war. Our approach to logistics recognizes and accepts war as a complex, uncertain, disorderly, and time-competitive clash of wills and seeks to provide the commander with the physical means to win in this environment. We seek logistics capabilities that extend our operational limits and that allow us to anticipate requirements while remaining flexible, adaptable, and responsive to the changing conditions in the battlespace. Marine logistics capabilities are based upon our warfighting philosophy of maneuver warfare. Our logistics support and enhance the conduct of operations which are oriented on the enemy, have a specific focus of effort, are conducted in accordance with the commander's intent, and help generate and maintain a high tempo of operations. Marine logistics are expeditionary in nature and naval in character. They are built on core capabilities at the strategic, operational, tactical levels; they are conducted through integrated and flexible planning and the exercise of responsive command and control. People are the foundation of Marine logistics. Marine logistics depends upon the exercise of leadership, discipline, attention to detail, and responsiveness by both the users of the logistics system and the persons who work within that system. Our doctrine, education, training, organization, procedures, and equipment provide the means for implementing Marine logistics. These components of our logistics capability reflect the unique requirements of maneuver warfare and our expeditionary nature. Together with our personnel, they provide a common basis for the conduct of effective logistic activities across the range of military operations.

The Nature of Logistics

1. British Army Doctrine Publication, Volume 3, *Logistics* (June 1996) p. 1-2.

2. LtGen Alfred M. Gray, Jr., "Training the Fleet Marine Force," *Marine Corps Gazette* (July 1987) p. 15. Gen A. M. Gray, Jr., was 29th Commandant of the Marine Corps.

3. Joint Pub 1-02, *Department of Defense Dictionary of Military and Associated Terms* (March 1994) p. 221.

4. Hans von Seeckt, *Gedanken eines Soldaten* (Leipzig: Hase & Koehler, 1936) pp. 159–63.

5. "The fact that in the study of the theory of war a variety of activities and functions are grouped together under the broad title of 'logistics' does not necessarily mean that all of these functions should be grouped under 'the logistic division' or any similar single title in fleet, army, theater, or service organization, or in the administration or operation of military services or forces," FMFRP 12-14, *Logistics in the National Defense* (April 1989) p. 9.

6. Complex systems and complexity is discussed more fully in MCDP 6, *Command and Control* (October 1996) pp. 44–47. For additional reading on complex (adaptive) systems: See M. Mitchell Waldrop, *Complexity: The Emerging Science at the Edge of Order and Chaos* (New York: Simon & Schuster, 1992); Roger Lewin, *Complexity: Life on the Edge of Chaos* (New York: Macmillan, 1992); or Kevin Kelly, *Out of Control: The New Biology of*

Machines: The Rise of Neo-Biological Civilization (Reading, MA: Addison-Wesley, 1994).

7.   David J. Frum, *Logistical Factors in the Fall of South Vietnam* (Masters Thesis, Yale University, 1982) passim.

8.   This base (designated Al Khanjar) covered 11,280 acres and contained enough food, water, fuel, and ammunition to support 2 divisions for 15 days. In addition, the base had the third largest Navy hospital in the world at that time. The base was created in response to a change in the MEF's operations plan which projected a simultaneous attack by two Marine divisions. Work began on the base on 6 Feb 1991 and was completed 14 days later, 4 days before the start of the ground war. For a detailed description, see BGen Charles C. Krulak's article "A War of Logistics," *Proceedings* (November, 1991) pp. 55–57.

9.   For a full account of this operation see Col James L. Jones' article "Operation Provide Comfort: Humanitarian and Security Assistance in Northern Iraq," *Marine Corps Gazette* (November 1991) pp. 98–107.

10.   The best short description of the relationship between the Inchon landing and the North Korean logistics system can be found in Kenneth Macksey, *For Want of a Nail: The Impact on War of Logistics and Communications* (London: Brassey's, 1989) pp. 160–164. For a more extensive treatment, see Charles Schrader, *Communist Logistics in the Korean War* (Westport, CT: Praeger Publishers, A Division of Greenwood Press, 1995).

11. For a full discussion of the human dimension in war as well as other characteristics of war discussed in this section, see MCDP 1 (formerly FMFM 1), *Warfighting*, chapter 1.

12. Steve R. Waddell, *United States Army Logistics: the Normandy Campaign, 1944* (Westport, CT: Greenwood Press, 1994) p. 131.

13. The best short discussion of the Chinese situation in December of 1950 is Lynn Montross' and Capt (USMC) Nicholas A. Canzona's *The Chosin Reservoir Campaign, Volume III* of *U.S. Marine Operations in Korea, 1950-1953*, (Washington, DC: Headquarters, U.S. Marine Corps, 1957). For the details of United Nations logistics, the best sources are contemporary articles published in such journals as *Marine Corps Gazette, Military Review, Proceedings, Quartermaster Review,* and *Ordnance.* For Chinese efforts to adapt their logistic system during the Korean war, see Shu Guangs Zhang, *Mao's Military Romanticism, China and the Korean War, 1950-1953* (Lawrence, KS: University Press of Kansas, 1995) pp. 165–176.

14. Waddell, p. 131.

15. The discussion of logistics in North Africa in World War II is taken from the manuscript of *Inside the Afrika Korps*, edited by Bruce Gudmundsson, to be published by Greenhill Books, London, in 1997.

Logistics Theory

1. Naval Doctrine Publication 4, *Naval Logistics* (January 1995) p. 36.

2. Col S. L. A. Marshall, *The Soldier's Load and the Mobility of a Nation* (Quantico, VA: The Marine Corps Association, 1980) pp. 3–4.

3. For a full discussion of the evolution of logistics, see Martin van Creveld, *Supplying War: Logistics from Wallenstein to Patton* (New York: Cambridge University Press, 1977).

4. J. F. C. Fuller, *The Conduct of War, 1789-1961; A Study of the French, Industrial, and Russian Revolutions on War and Its Conduct* (Minerva Press, 1968) pp. 22–23.

5. For a full account of Forward Operating Base Cobra, see Tom Taylor, *Lightning in the Storm: The 101st Air Assault Division in the Gulf War* (New York: Hippocrene Books, 1994).

6. Edward Hagerman, *The American Civil War and the Origins of Modern Warfare: Ideas, Organization, and Field Command* (Bloomington, IN: Indiana University Press, 1992) pp. 246–247.

7. FMFRP 12-34-V, *History of U.S. Marine Corps Operations in World War II: Victory and Occupation, Volume V* (August 1989) p. 70.

8.   Charles R. Smith, *Angels From the Sea: Relief Operations in Bangladesh, 1991* (Washington, DC: Headquarters, U.S. Marine Corps, History and Museums Division, 1995).

9.   Charles W. Koburger, Jr., *Sea Power in the Falklands*, Chapter 7, "Logistics" (New York: Praeger, 1983).

10. For a full discussion of the importance of command and control and the makeup and functioning of a command and control system, see MCDP 6, chapter 1.

11. FMFRP 12-14, p. 153.

12. Kenneth W. Condit, "Marine Supply in Korea," *Marine Corps Gazette* (January 1953) pp. 48–55.

13. Waddell, p. 145.

14. For a full discussion of efficiency and effectiveness in military logistics, see FMFRP 12-14, p. 317 and William G. Pagonis with Jeffery L. Cruikshank, *Moving Mountains: Lessons in Leadership and Logistics from the Gulf War* (Boston, MA: Harvard Business School Press, 1992) p. 150.

15. Cpl Joseph F. O'Brien, "Logistics Roots," *Logistics Spectrum* (Summer 1990) pp. 7–11.

Creating Effective Logistics

1.   Gen Carl E. Mundy, Jr. "Naval Expeditionary Forces: Stepping Lightly," *Marine Corps Gazette* (February 1993) p. 14. Gen C. E. Mundy, Jr., was 30th Commandant of the Marine Corps.

2.   BGen James A. Brabham, "Training, Education Were the Keys," *Proceedings* (November 1991) pp. 51–54. MajGen Brabham was Commanding General, 1st Service Support Group, during Operation Desert Shield/Desert Storm.

3.   For a full discussion of maneuver warfare, see MCDP 1 (formerly FMFM 1), *Warfighting*, chapter 4.

4.   From an unpublished work, *The Logistics of the British Expeditionary Force, 1914-1918*, chapter 7, by Ian Brown. For a description of the paralysis of the operational command system, see Tim Travers, *The Killing Ground: The British Army, the Western Front, and the Emergence of Modern Warfare, 1900-1918* (London: Allen & Unwin, 1987).

5.   Per Joint Pub 4-0, *Doctrine for Logistic Support of Joint Operations* (January 1995) p. I-7, each Service is **responsible for the logistic support of its own force**, except when logistic support is otherwise provided for by agreements with national agencies or allies, or by assignments to common, joint, or cross-servicing.

6.   The levels of planning are discussed in detail in chapter 2 of MCDP 5, *Planning*.

7. For a complete discussion of the relationship between planning and command and control, see MCDP 5, chapter 1, and MCDP 6, chapter 3.

8. For a full discussion of the snowball effect, see FMFRP 12-14, pp. 102–113. For further discussion of the role of discipline in logistics, see FMFRP 12-14, pp. 185–195.

9. LtCol H. T. Hayden and LtCol G. I. Wilson, "The Tail that Wags the Dog," *Proceedings* (October 1990) p. 52.

10. See George C. Thorpe, *Pure Logistics: The Science of War Preparation* (Washington, DC: National Defense University Press, 1986) p. 24 for a discussion on the supply of Sherman's army during the Atlanta campaign.

11. Hayden and Wilson, p. 52.

12. The lessons learned from the use of this particular organizational arrangement are being incorporated into a concept for operational-level logistic support. The organization which provides operational-level logistic support will be designated the Marine Logistics Command (MLC).

www.ingramcontent.com/pod-product-compliance
Lightning Source LLC
Chambersburg PA
CBHW070706290526
45790CB00001B/465